USA TODAY
SNAPSHOTS®

MORE THAN 2,000 FACTS AND FIGURES ON LIFE, LOVE, MONEY, AND SPORTS!

A miscellany by the editors of USA TODAY®,
America's most read newspaper

STERLING INNOVATION
An imprint of Sterling Publishing Co., Inc.

New York / London
www.sterlingpublishing.com

STERLING, the Sterling logo, STERLING INNOVATION, and the Sterling
Innovation logo are registered trademarks of Sterling Publishing Co., Inc.

USA TODAY®, its logo, and associated graphics are federally registered trademarks.
All rights are reserved. All USA TODAY® text, graphics, and photographs are used
pursuant to a license and may not be reproduced, distributed, or otherwise used
without the express written consent of Gannett, Co., Inc.

Library of Congress Cataloging-in-Publication Data Available

2 4 6 8 10 9 7 5 3 1

Published by Sterling Publishing Co., Inc.
387 Park Avenue South, New York, NY 10016
© 2009 by Sterling Publishing Co., Inc.
Distributed in Canada by Sterling Publishing
c/o Canadian Manda Group, 165 Dufferin Street
Toronto, Ontario, Canada M6K 3H6
Distributed in the United Kingdom by GMC Distribution Services
Castle Place, 166 High Street, Lewes, East Sussex, England BN7 1XU
Distributed in Australia by Capricorn Link (Australia) Pty. Ltd.
P.O. Box 704, Windsor, NSW 2756, Australia

Printed in China
All rights reserved

Sterling ISBN 978-1-4027-6438-7

**All of the USA TODAY Snapshots® in this book appeared in
USA TODAY® between January 1, 2005, and October 30, 2008.**

For information about custom editions, special sales, premium and
corporate purchases, please contact Sterling Special Sales
Department at 800-805-5489 or specialsales@sterlingpublishing.com

TABLE OF CONTENTS

FOREWORD	6
EARNING	9
SPENDING	41
SAVING	83
ROMANCE	119
FAMILY	143
HOME	174
LEISURE	213
TECHNOLOGY	263
BUSINESS	297
EDUCATION	343
SPORTS	389
HOLIDAYS	425
HEALTH	461

Foreword

There are several interesting facts regarding USA TODAY Snapshots. One is that tracing their origin and finding the one person responsible for the idea of a Snapshot has been surprisingly difficult. In 2007, on our 25th anniversary as a newspaper, we tried to identify the creator. Not even the paper's founder could remember their origin. We finally came to the conclusion that the paper's first executive editor had come up with the idea—though he had suggested we only produce one Snapshot per day.

Luckily for our readers, who have consistently rated Snapshots as one of their favorite USA TODAY features, the newspaper has always had four Snapshots per day—one on each section's front page. Snapshots are intended to entertain readers while giving them a sense of the statistics that shape our nation. Each one tells us something interesting about ourselves and those around us.

Researchers, reporters, and editors in each of the four primary departments (News, Money, Sports, and Life) account for most of the ideas and research for Snapshots.

Inspiration comes from a variety of sources: official reports, such as the census; results of surveys and polls, such as Gallup; or original reporting. After research is done, the results pass through an editor to a graphics artist, who illustrates the Snapshot and brings it to life. On average, a Snapshot takes the artist about three to four hours to complete. About half that time is spent conceptualizing the illustration.

When the stars align correctly, the perfect Snapshot will have a news peg. This means it illustrates something that is currently in the news, capturing the feeling of the specific moment in which we are living.

Over the course of our history, USA TODAY has produced an estimated 26,000 Snapshots. So always look for one of our staff members to be on your trivia contest team!

Each of the Snapshots in this book was selected so that you can compare your life and your thoughts to those represented by the numbers in the Snapshot. We hope that you enjoy reading them as much as we have enjoyed producing them.

Richard Curtis
Managing Editor, Design, USA TODAY®

■ Earning

When it comes to earning a paycheck, what kind of employee are you? Do you call in sick only to head to the beach? Do you dress like your boss to gain his or her respect? Are you in the majority or the minority of workers when it comes to understanding how to read your paycheck?

What concerns you most? Do you worry about your retirement? More than you worry about being laid off? Or does outsourcing weigh heavy on your mind? Do you think an Ivy League degree would get you further than one from a state school? Are you expecting a raise at your next review? Is that normal? What percentage of workers is concerned about the same things you are?

Where do you fit in?

USA TODAY Snapshots®

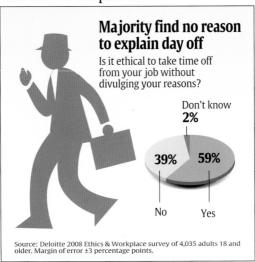

Majority find no reason to explain day off

Is it ethical to take time off from your job without divulging your reasons?

Don't know
2%

39% **59%**

No Yes

Source: Deloitte 2008 Ethics & Workplace survey of 4,035 adults 18 and older. Margin of error ±3 percentage points.

By Jae Yang and Keith Simmons, USA TODAY

USA TODAY Snapshots®

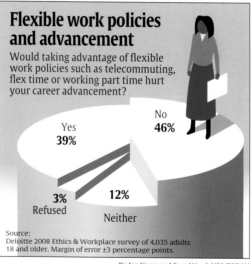

Flexible work policies and advancement

Would taking advantage of flexible work policies such as telecommuting, flex time or working part time hurt your career advancement?

Yes
39%

No
46%

3%
Refused

12%
Neither

Source:
Deloitte 2008 Ethics & Workplace survey of 4,035 adults 18 and older. Margin of error ±3 percentage points.

By Jae Yang and Sam Ward, USA TODAY

USA TODAY Snapshots®

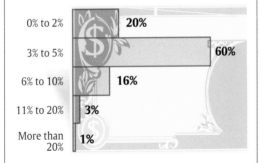

Most expect 3% to 5% pay raise

How much of a salary increase do you expect to get after your next review?

0% to 2%	**20%**
3% to 5%	**60%**
6% to 10%	**16%**
11% to 20%	**3%**
More than 20%	**1%**

Source: IABC survey of 3,370 workers. Weighted to actual population proportion.

By Jae Yang and Robert W. Ahrens, USA TODAY

USA TODAY Snapshots®

Trading places

Do you think you could do as good a job or better than your boss does if you switched positions for a day?

Yes **43%**

No **25%**

Not sure **33%**

Source:
Yahoo HotJobs survey of 1,271 employees.
Margin of error ±3 percentage points.

By Jae Yang and Sam Ward, USA TODAY

USA TODAY Snapshots®

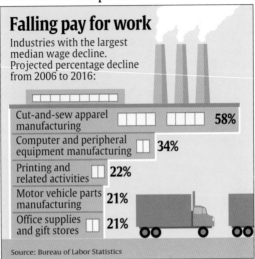

Falling pay for work

Industries with the largest
median wage decline.
Projected percentage decline
from 2006 to 2016:

Cut-and-sew apparel manufacturing **58%**

Computer and peripheral equipment manufacturing **34%**

Printing and related activities **22%**

Motor vehicle parts manufacturing **21%**

Office supplies and gift stores **21%**

Source: Bureau of Labor Statistics

By Jae Yang and Alejandro Gonzalez, USA TODAY

USA TODAY Snapshots®

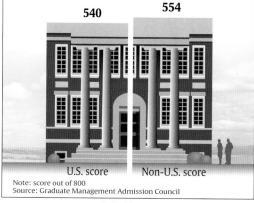

The world of business school

Mean General Management Admission Test (GMAT) scores in USA and abroad, 2006–2007:

540   554

U.S. score   Non-U.S. score

Note: score out of 800
Source: Graduate Management Admission Council

By David Stuckey and Karl Gelles, USA TODAY

USA TODAY Snapshots®

Salaries on the rise

Industries with the largest median wage growth.
Projected percentage growth from 2006 to 2016:

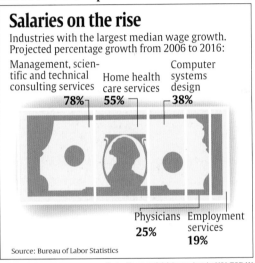

Management, scientific and technical consulting services
78%

Home health care services
55%

Computer systems design
38%

Physicians
25%

Employment services
19%

Source: Bureau of Labor Statistics

By Jae Yang and Adrienne Lewis, USA TODAY

USA TODAY Snapshots®

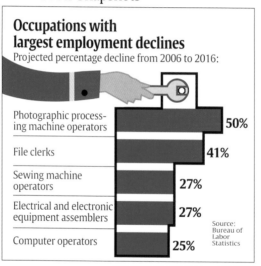

Occupations with largest employment declines

Projected percentage decline from 2006 to 2016:

Occupation	Percentage
Photographic processing machine operators	50%
File clerks	41%
Sewing machine operators	27%
Electrical and electronic equipment assemblers	27%
Computer operators	25%

Source: Bureau of Labor Statistics

By Jae Yang and Keith Simmons, USA TODAY

USA TODAY Snapshots®

Jobs women dominate

In the following fields, percentage of jobs filled by women:

Preschool and kindergarten teachers — **98%**

Travel agents — **77%**

Psychologists — **68%**

Tax preparers — **60%**

Source: Census Bureau

By David Stuckey and Sam Ward, USA TODAY

USA TODAY Snapshots®

Work and life balance motivates female entrepreneurs

Ninety-eight percent of female entrepreneurs are satisfied about owning a business regardless of the challenges. Major reasons for female entrepreneurs to start businesses:

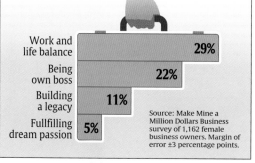

Work and life balance **29%**

Being own boss **22%**

Building a legacy **11%**

Fullfilling dream passion **5%**

Source: Make Mine a Million Dollars Business survey of 1,162 female business owners. Margin of error ±3 percentage points.

By Jae Yang and Alejandro Gonzalez, USA TODAY

USA TODAY Snapshots®

Income gap persists between older men, women

Median income in 2004 of men and women ages 65 and older:

$21,102

$12,080

Men

Women

Source: AARP

By David Stuckey and Alejandro Gonzalez, USA TODAY

20

USA TODAY Snapshots®

Executives oppose legislation to end gender pay gap

Does the inequality of women's pay, 77 cents for every dollar a man makes, need to be addressed through laws?

No
76%

Yes
24%

Source: BlueSteps.com/AESC survey of 320 executives

By Jae Yang and Sam Ward, USA TODAY

USA TODAY Snapshots®

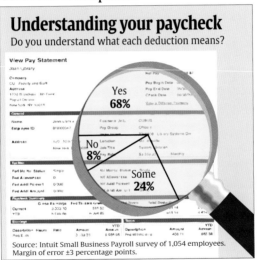

Understanding your paycheck

Do you understand what each deduction means?

Yes
68%

No
8%

Some
24%

Source: Intuit Small Business Payroll survey of 1,054 employees.
Margin of error ±3 percentage points.

By Jae Yang and Adrienne Lewis, USA TODAY

USA TODAY Snapshots®

Disappointment at pay time

Percentage of U.S. workers who were satisfied with their pay raise:

57%

53%

42%

2000

2003

2006

Source: Sibson Consulting 2006 Rewards of Work study of 1,238 workers. Margin of error ±3 percentage points.

By Jae Yang and Alejandro Gonzalez, USA TODAY

USA TODAY Snapshots®

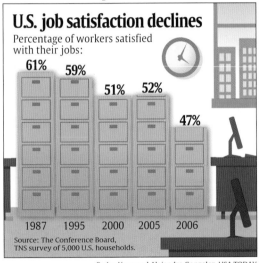

U.S. job satisfaction declines

Percentage of workers satisfied with their jobs:

61% — 1987
59% — 1995
51% — 2000
52% — 2005
47% — 2006

Source: The Conference Board, TNS survey of 5,000 U.S. households.

By Jae Yang and Alejandro Gonzalez, USA TODAY

USA TODAY Snapshots®

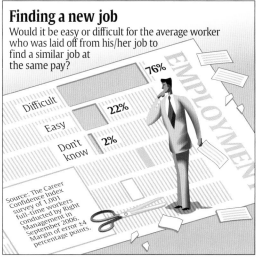

Finding a new job

Would it be easy or difficult for the average worker who was laid off from his/her job to find a similar job at the same pay?

Difficult — 76%

Easy — 22%

Don't know — 2%

Source: The Career Confidence Index survey of 1,001 full-time workers conducted by Right Management in September 2006. Margin of error ±4 percentage points.

By Jae Yang and Dave Merrill, USA TODAY

USA TODAY Snapshots®

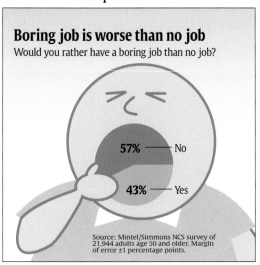

Boring job is worse than no job
Would you rather have a boring job than no job?

57% —— No

43% —— Yes

Source: Mintel/Simmons NCS survey of
21,944 adults age 50 and older. Margin
of error ±1 percentage points.

By Jae Yang and Keith Simmons, USA TODAY

USA TODAY Snapshots®

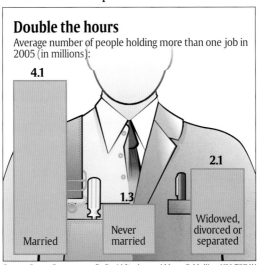

Double the hours

Average number of people holding more than one job in 2005 (in millions):

4.1

2.1

1.3

Married

Never married

Widowed, divorced or separated

Source: Census Bureau   By David Stuckey and Marcy E. Mullins, USA TODAY

USA TODAY Snapshots®

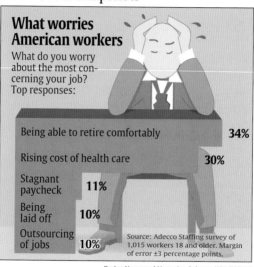

What worries American workers

What do you worry about the most concerning your job? Top responses:

Being able to retire comfortably	**34%**
Rising cost of health care	**30%**
Stagnant paycheck	**11%**
Being laid off	**10%**
Outsourcing of jobs	**10%**

Source: Adecco Staffing survey of 1,015 workers 18 and older. Margin of error ±3 percentage points.

By Jae Yang and Veronica Salazar, USA TODAY

USA TODAY Snapshots®

Security clearance boosts salary

Average salary with clearance

$67,429

Average salary without clearance

$51,147

Source: ClearanceJobs.com

By Jae Yang and Adrienne Lewis, USA TODAY

USA TODAY Snapshots®

Is university prestige important when job hunting?

Financial executives are divided on whether the prestige of an entry-level job candidate's university is important.

Important
51%

Not important
49%

Source: Accountemps survey of 1,400 chief financial officers. Margin of error ±3 percentage points.

By Jae Yang and Veronica Salazar, USA TODAY

30

USA TODAY Snapshots®

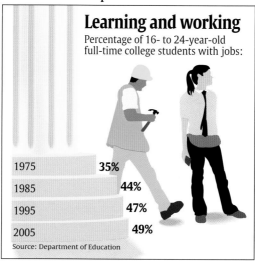

Learning and working

Percentage of 16- to 24-year-old
full-time college students with jobs:

1975	**35%**
1985	**44%**
1995	**47%**
2005	**49%**

Source: Department of Education

By David Stuckey and Robert W. Ahrens, USA TODAY

USA TODAY Snapshots®

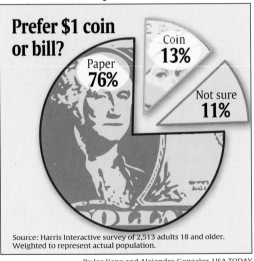

Prefer $1 coin or bill?

Paper **76%**

Coin **13%**

Not sure **11%**

Source: Harris Interactive survey of 2,513 adults 18 and older. Weighted to represent actual population.

By Jae Yang and Alejandro Gonzalez, USA TODAY

USA TODAY Snapshots®

Hurdles to job-seeking

Forty-two percent of surveyed respondents would like a new job but are not actively looking. What keeps employees from looking for another job?

Top responses:

Proving myself to a new employer is hard	36%
Procrastination	27%
Being happy with current work-life balance	27%
Not wanting to let down current bosses	26%
Short and easy commute	26%

Note: Multiple responses allowed.

Source: Yahoo HotJobs survey of 1,271 employees. Margin of error ±3 parentage points.

By Jae Yang and Sam Ward, USA TODAY

USA TODAY Snapshots®

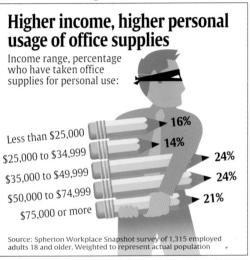

Higher income, higher personal usage of office supplies

Income range, percentage who have taken office supplies for personal use:

Less than $25,000 ▸ 16%

$25,000 to $34,999 ▸ 14%

$35,000 to $49,999 ▸ 24%

$50,000 to $74,999 ▸ 24%

$75,000 or more ▸ 21%

Source: Spherion Workplace Snapshot survey of 1,315 employed adults 18 and older. Weighted to represent actual population

By Jae Yang and Karl Gelles, USA TODAY

USA TODAY Snapshots®

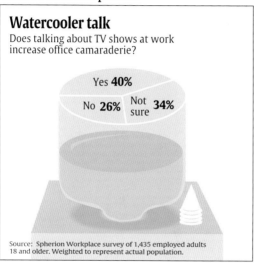

Watercooler talk

Does talking about TV shows at work increase office camaraderie?

Yes **40%**

No **26%** Not sure **34%**

Source: Spherion Workplace survey of 1,435 employed adults 18 and older. Weighted to represent actual population.

By Jae Yang and Adrienne Lewis, USA TODAY

USA TODAY Snapshots®

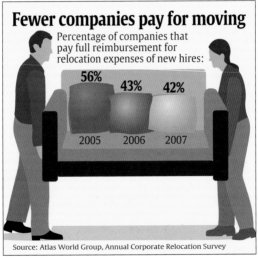

Fewer companies pay for moving

Percentage of companies that pay full reimbursement for relocation expenses of new hires:

56% — 2005
43% — 2006
42% — 2007

Source: Atlas World Group, Annual Corporate Relocation Survey

By David Stuckey and Alejandro Gonzalez, USA TODAY

USA TODAY Snapshots®

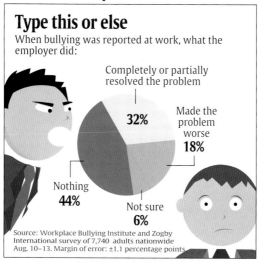

Type this or else

When bullying was reported at work, what the employer did:

Completely or partially resolved the problem

32%

Made the problem worse **18%**

Nothing **44%**

Not sure **6%**

Source: Workplace Bullying Institute and Zogby International survey of 7,740 adults nationwide Aug. 10–13. Margin of error: ±1.1 percentage points

By Melanie Eversley and Veronica Salazar, USA TODAY

USA TODAY Snapshots®

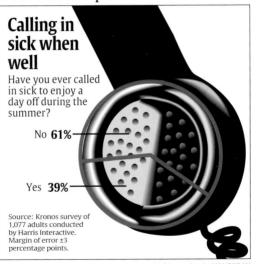

Calling in sick when well

Have you ever called in sick to enjoy a day off during the summer?

No **61%**

Yes **39%**

Source: Kronos survey of 1,077 adults conducted by Harris Interactive. Margin of error ±3 percentage points.

By Jae Yang and Adrienne Lewis, USA TODAY

USA TODAY Snapshots®

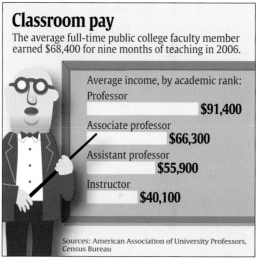

Classroom pay

The average full-time public college faculty member earned $68,400 for nine months of teaching in 2006.

Average income, by academic rank:

Professor
$91,400

Associate professor
$66,300

Assistant professor
$55,900

Instructor
$40,100

Sources: American Association of University Professors, Census Bureau

By David Stuckey and Alejandro Gonzalez, USA TODAY

■ Spending

One thing we all seem to have in common: We wish we didn't spend so much money. But are you spending more or less than the Joneses? Maybe you're trying to cut back—what are you least willing to give up? Dinners out? Vacations away? Nights at the movies? Italian shoes?

When it comes to paying the bills, where is your money going? Are you alone in finding shopping stressful? Do you pay more or less than average for daily parking? Are you the only one changing your habits to accommodate ghastly gasoline prices? And is everyone misplacing those plastic gift cards?

How do you fare?

USA TODAY Snapshots®

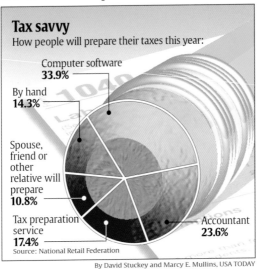

Tax savvy

How people will prepare their taxes this year:

Computer software
33.9%

By hand
14.3%

Spouse, friend or other relative will prepare
10.8%

Tax preparation service
17.4%

Accountant
23.6%

Source: National Retail Federation

By David Stuckey and Marcy E. Mullins, USA TODAY

USA TODAY Snapshots®

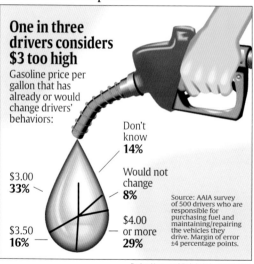

One in three drivers considers $3 too high

Gasoline price per gallon that has already or would change drivers' behaviors:

Don't know **14%**

Would not change **8%**

$3.00 **33%**

$4.00 or more **29%**

$3.50 **16%**

Source: AAIA survey of 500 drivers who are responsible for purchasing fuel and maintaining/repairing the vehicles they drive. Margin of error ±4 percentage points.

By Jae Yang and Bob Laird, USA TODAY

USA TODAY Snapshots®

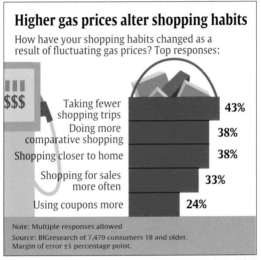

Higher gas prices alter shopping habits

How have your shopping habits changed as a result of fluctuating gas prices? Top responses:

Taking fewer shopping trips — 43%

Doing more comparative shopping — 38%

Shopping closer to home — 38%

Shopping for sales more often — 33%

Using coupons more — 24%

Note: Multiple responses allowed

Source: BIGresearch of 7,479 consumers 18 and older. Margin of error ±1 percentage point.

By Jae Yang and Sam Ward, USA TODAY

USA TODAY Snapshots®

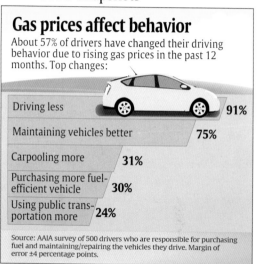

Gas prices affect behavior

About 57% of drivers have changed their driving behavior due to rising gas prices in the past 12 months. Top changes:

Driving less	91%
Maintaining vehicles better	75%
Carpooling more	31%
Purchasing more fuel-efficient vehicle	30%
Using public transportation more	24%

Source: AAIA survey of 500 drivers who are responsible for purchasing fuel and maintaining/repairing the vehicles they drive. Margin of error ±4 percentage points.

By Jae Yang and Robert W. Ahrens, USA TODAY

USA TODAY Snapshots®

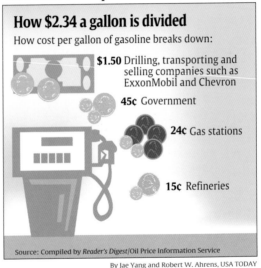

How $2.34 a gallon is divided

How cost per gallon of gasoline breaks down:

$1.50 Drilling, transporting and selling companies such as ExxonMobil and Chevron

45¢ Government

24¢ Gas stations

15¢ Refineries

Source: Compiled by *Reader's Digest*/Oil Price Information Service

By Jae Yang and Robert W. Ahrens, USA TODAY

USA TODAY Snapshots®

Average new vehicle retail selling price

$21,900

$28,450

$20,000
$10,000
0

1996   2006

Source: National Automobile Dealers Association

By David Stuckey and Karl Gelles, USA TODAY

USA TODAY Snapshots®

Dealership receipts

Average new and used car dealer sales, per establishment, in 2007:

$24 million
New car

$2 million
Used car

Source: Census Bureau   By David Stuckey and Karl Gelles, USA TODAY

USA TODAY Snapshots®

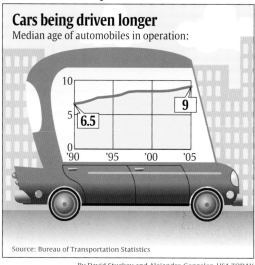

Cars being driven longer
Median age of automobiles in operation:

6.5

9

'90   '95   '00   '05

Source: Bureau of Transportation Statistics

By David Stuckey and Alejandro Gonzalez, USA TODAY

USA TODAY Snapshots®

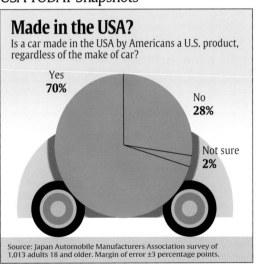

Made in the USA?

Is a car made in the USA by Americans a U.S. product, regardless of the make of car?

Yes
70%

No
28%

Not sure
2%

Source: Japan Automobile Manufacturers Association survey of 1,013 adults 18 and older. Margin of error ±3 percentage points.

By Jae Yang and Sam Ward, USA TODAY

USA TODAY Snapshots®

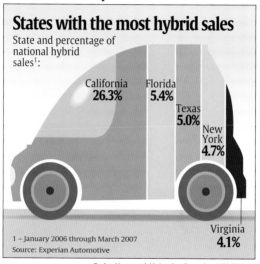

States with the most hybrid sales

State and percentage of national hybrid sales[1]:

California
26.3%

Florida
5.4%

Texas
5.0%

New York
4.7%

Virginia
4.1%

1 – January 2006 through March 2007
Source: Experian Automotive

By Jae Yang and Alejandro Gonzalez, USA TODAY

USA TODAY Snapshots®

Cities with costliest parking
Daily parking rate:

$42 — New York, Midtown
$34 — New York, downtown
$33 — Boston
$32 — Honolulu
$27 — San Francisco

Source: Colliers International

By Jae Yang and Alejandro Gonzalez, USA TODAY

USA TODAY Snapshots®

Dining out is hardest to give up

What would you be least willing to give up or cut back on each month to save more for retirement? Top categories:

Dining out — 31%
Travel — 18%
Clothes — 17%
Entertainment — 15%
Sporting event — 10%

Source: ShareBuilder survey of 2,033 adults 21 and older. Margin of error±2 percentage points.

By Jae Yang and Robert W. Ahrens, USA TODAY

USA TODAY Snapshots®

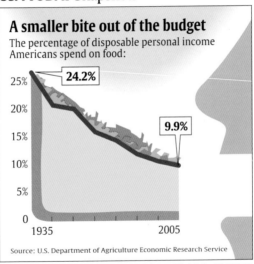

A smaller bite out of the budget

The percentage of disposable personal income Americans spend on food:

Source: U.S. Department of Agriculture Economic Research Service

By Tracey Wong Briggs and Karl Gelles, USA TODAY

USA TODAY Snapshots®

The cost of organic food

Percentage of parents living with kids under 18 who say organic food is not worth the extra cost:

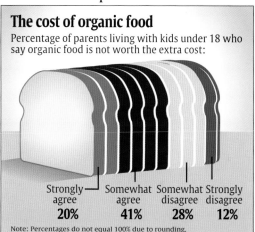

Strongly agree	Somewhat agree	Somewhat disagree	Strongly disagree
20%	41%	28%	12%

Note: Percentages do not equal 100% due to rounding.
Source: Harris Interactive online survey for SuperTarget of 496 adults living with children under 18, between March 23-27. Margin of error, ±6.5 percentage points.

By Mary Cadden and Alejandro Gonzalez, USA TODAY

USA TODAY Snapshots®

Women's most-trusted shopping advisers

Friends/family 45%
Online user reviews 13%
News media 11%
Advertising 7%
Manufacturer websites 5%
Retail websites 4%
Salespeople 1%
Other 14%

Source: *Consumer Reports* National Research Center online survey of 1,264 women, May 22–24, for *ShopSmart* magazine. Margin of error ± 2.8 percentage points

By Mary Cadden and Dave Merrill, USA TODAY

USA TODAY Snapshots®

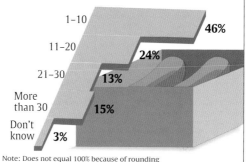

How many pairs of shoes women have in their closets

1–10 — **46%**

11–20 — **24%**

21–30 — **13%**

More than 30 — **15%**

Don't know — **3%**

Note: Does not equal 100% because of rounding

Source: *The Consumer Reports* National Research Center telephone survey of 1,057 women (June 29–July 2) for *ShopSmart* magazine. Margin of error is ±3.1 percentage points.

By Mary Cadden and Adrienne Lewis, USA TODAY

USA TODAY Snapshots®

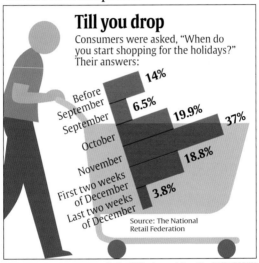

Till you drop

Consumers were asked, "When do you start shopping for the holidays?" Their answers:

Before September	14%
September	6.5%
October	19.9%
November	37%
First two weeks of December	18.8%
Last two weeks of December	3.8%

Source: The National Retail Federation

By David Stuckey and Sam Ward, USA TODAY

58

USA TODAY Snapshots®

Gift of shopping is appealing

Gift cards are gradually gaining popularity as a holiday gift, ranking as the second-most-popular item after clothing this year. Top three features of gift cards for holiday shoppers:

66%

I want the receiver to choose his/her own gift

49%

My holiday shopping is easy and less time-consuming

38%

I can buy at the last minute

Note: Multiple responses allowed

Source: American Express Gift Card survey of 1,013 adults 18 and older. Margin of error ±3 percentage points.

By Jae Yang and Adrienne Lewis, USA TODAY

USA TODAY Snapshots®

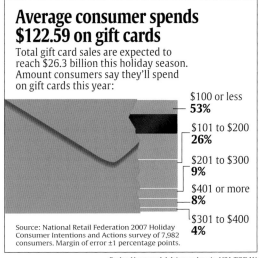

Average consumer spends $122.59 on gift cards

Total gift card sales are expected to reach $26.3 billion this holiday season. Amount consumers say they'll spend on gift cards this year:

$100 or less
53%

$101 to $200
26%

$201 to $300
9%

$401 or more
8%

$301 to $400
4%

Source: National Retail Federation 2007 Holiday Consumer Intentions and Actions survey of 7,982 consumers. Margin of error ±1 percentage points.

By Jae Yang and Adrienne Lewis, USA TODAY

USA TODAY Snapshots®

Many consumers skip small print

When making a purchase in a store, do you read service contracts, warranties and return or exchange policies? Percentage who said yes:

Return or exchange policies
71%

Extended warranties
57%

Service contracts
53%

See back for return policy

Source: Better Business Bureau survey of 1,000 adults age 18 and older. Margin of error ±3 percentage points.

By Jae Yang and Veronica Salazar, USA TODAY

USA TODAY Snapshots®

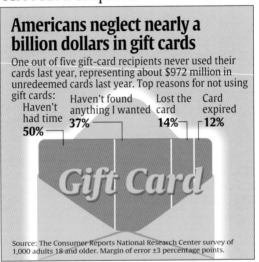

Americans neglect nearly a billion dollars in gift cards

One out of five gift-card recipients never used their cards last year, representing about $972 million in unredeemed cards last year. Top reasons for not using gift cards:

Haven't had time
50%

Haven't found anything I wanted
37%

Lost the card
14%

Card expired
12%

Gift Card

Source: The Consumer Reports National Research Center survey of 1,000 adults 18 and older. Margin of error ±3 percentage points.

By Jae Yang and Adrienne Lewis, USA TODAY

USA TODAY Snapshots®

How far in advance gift-givers typically shop

The same day as giving it **4%**

A month or longer **8%**

Within a month **12%**

Within a week **41%**

Within three weeks **12%**

Within two weeks **23%**

Source: Harris Interactive online study via QuickQuery for Gifts.com of 2,730 adults, April 20–24. Margin of error, ± 3 percentage points.

By Mary Cadden and Suzy Parker, USA TODAY

USA TODAY Snapshots®

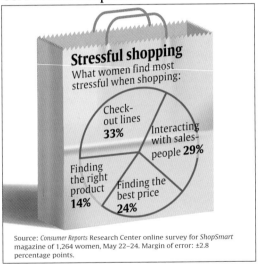

Stressful shopping

What women find most stressful when shopping:

- Check-out lines **33%**
- Interacting with sales-people **29%**
- Finding the right product **14%**
- Finding the best price **24%**

Source: *Consumer Reports* Research Center online survey for *ShopSmart* magazine of 1,264 women, May 22–24. Margin of error: ±2.8 percentage points.

By Mary Cadden and Karl Gelles, USA TODAY

USA TODAY Snapshots®

Physical stores' advantage

Sixty-seven percent of survey respondents favor shopping at stores vs. online. Main reasons to shop at stores:

Need to see or try on item

51%

Need to have product sooner than the time it takes to ship

13%

Better price

12%

Avoid shipping charges

12%

Source: Accenture Retail & CGS Innovation survey of 602 adults 18 and older. Margin of error ±3 percentage points.

By Jae Yang and Alejandro Gonzalez, USA TODAY

USA TODAY Snapshots®

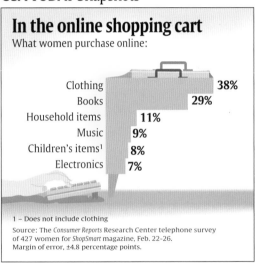

In the online shopping cart

What women purchase online:

Clothing	**38%**
Books	**29%**
Household items	**11%**
Music	**9%**
Children's items[1]	**8%**
Electronics	**7%**

1 – Does not include clothing

Source: The *Consumer Reports* Research Center telephone survey of 427 women for *ShopSmart* magazine, Feb. 22-26. Margin of error, ±4.8 percentage points.

By Mary Cadden and Robert W. Ahrens, USA TODAY

USA TODAY Snapshots®

Consumers' product reviews influential

A survey finds 62% of consumers read consumer-written product reviews on the Internet when they choose products to purchase. Product purchases most influenced by consumer reviews:

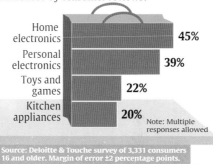

Home electronics **45%**

Personal electronics **39%**

Toys and games **22%**

Kitchen appliances **20%**

Note: Multiple responses allowed

Source: Deloitte & Touche survey of 3,331 consumers 16 and older. Margin of error ±2 percentage points.

By Jae Yang and Adrienne Lewis, USA TODAY

USA TODAY Snapshots®

Customer service plays big role in consumer loyalty

What has the biggest influence on your loyalty to a company?

Customer service **48%**

Product quality **37%**

Price **13%**

Brand name/ reputation **2%**

Source: Genesys Telecommunications Labs consumer survey of 500 adults 18 and older. Margin of error ±5 percentage points.

By Jae Yang and Alejandro Gonzalez, USA TODAY

USA TODAY Snapshots®

What annoys retail shoppers

Too little attention	**24%**
Too much attention	15%
Pressure to buy products	12%
Difficulty with returns	11%
Being treated rudely	10%

Source: Accenture's Institute for High Performance Business survey of 1,300 consumers. Margin of error: ±3 percentage points.

By Jae Yang and Karl Gelles, USA TODAY

USA TODAY Snapshots®

Cashless society

Do you think our society will someday operate without cash and checks and do all transactions electronically?

Yes
77%

No
21%

Not sure **2%**

Source: Visa/Yankelovich survey of 1,000 adults 18 and older.
Margin of error: ±5 percentage points.

By Jae Yang and Karl Gelles, USA TODAY

USA TODAY Snapshots®

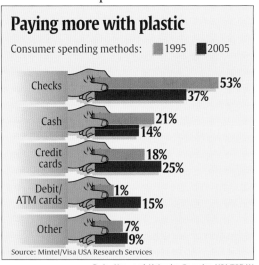

Paying more with plastic

Consumer spending methods: ■ 1995 ■ 2005

Checks **53%** **37%**

Cash **21%** **14%**

Credit cards **18%** **25%**

Debit/ATM cards **1%** **15%**

Other **7%** **9%**

Source: Mintel/Visa USA Research Services

By Jae Yang and Alejandro Gonzalez, USA TODAY

USA TODAY Snapshots®

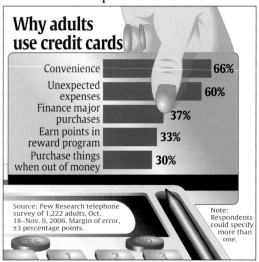

Why adults use credit cards

Convenience	66%
Unexpected expenses	60%
Finance major purchases	37%
Earn points in reward program	33%
Purchase things when out of money	30%

Source: Pew Research telephone survey of 1,222 adults, Oct. 18–Nov. 9, 2006. Margin of error, ±3 percentage points.

Note: Respondents could specify more than one.

By Mary Cadden and Marcy E. Mullins, USA TODAY

USA TODAY Snapshots®

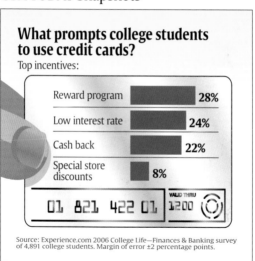

What prompts college students to use credit cards?

Top incentives:

Reward program	28%
Low interest rate	24%
Cash back	22%
Special store discounts	8%

01 821 422 01   VALID THRU 1200

Source: Experience.com 2006 College Life—Finances & Banking survey of 4,891 college students. Margin of error ±2 percentage points.

By Jae Yang and Keith Simmons, USA TODAY

USA TODAY Snapshots®

Paying off the plastic

Fifty-eight percent of adults have monthly credit card bills. Monthly bill-paying habits:

✓ Have regular credit card bills	**58%**
Pay credit card bill in full	**24%**
Make a credit card payment	**31%**
It depends	**3%**
✓ Do not have regular credit card expense	**41%**
✓ Don't know	**1%**

Source: Pew Research telephone survey of 2,000 adults, Oct. 18–Nov. 9, 2006. Margin of error, ±2.5 percentage points.

By Mary Cadden and Adrienne Lewis, USA TODAY

USA TODAY Snapshots®

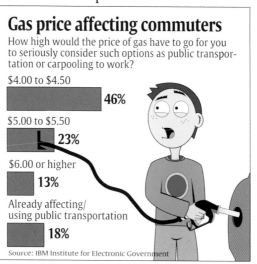

Gas price affecting commuters

How high would the price of gas have to go for you to seriously consider such options as public transportation or carpooling to work?

$4.00 to $4.50
46%

$5.00 to $5.50
23%

$6.00 or higher
13%

Already affecting/
using public transportation
18%

Source: IBM Institute for Electronic Government

By Jae Yang and Veronica Salazar, USA TODAY

USA TODAY Snapshots®

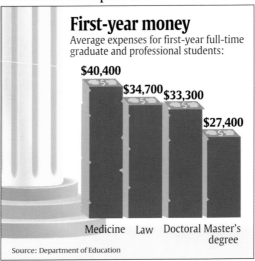

First-year money

Average expenses for first-year full-time graduate and professional students:

$40,400

$34,700

$33,300

$27,400

Medicine Law Doctoral Master's degree

Source: Department of Education

By David Stuckey and Robert W. Ahrens, USA TODAY

USA TODAY Snapshots®

Back-to-school shopping

How much do you plan to spend on back-to-school items this year? Average amounts:

Clothing and accessories
$231.80

Electronics and computer-related equipment
$129.24

School supplies
$94.02

Source: National Retail Federation 2007 Back-to-School Consumer Intentions and Actions survey of 8,290 shoppers conducted by BIGresearch.

Shoes
$108.42

By Jae Yang and Veronica Salazar, USA TODAY

USA TODAY Snapshots®

Oh! The taxes we pay

Per capita state taxes collected in 2005 averaged $2,189.84 across the USA. How they break down:

Sales and receipts	$1,051.42
Income	$875.23
Licenses	$144.33
Others	$80.49
Property[1]	$38.36

1 - does not include local or school district property taxes

Source: Census Bureau

By Sam Ward, USA TODAY

USA TODAY Snapshots®

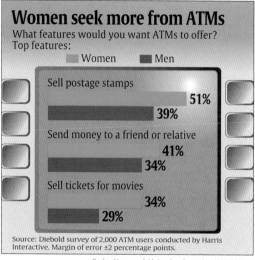

Women seek more from ATMs

What features would you want ATMs to offer?
Top features:

Women Men

Sell postage stamps
51%
39%

Send money to a friend or relative
41%
34%

Sell tickets for movies
34%
29%

Source: Diebold survey of 2,000 ATM users conducted by Harris Interactive. Margin of error ±2 percentage points.

By Jae Yang and Alejandro Gonzalez, USA TODAY

USA TODAY Snapshots®

Tax refund spending

About 70% of survey respondents expect a tax refund this year. Top ways the refunds will be spent:

Savings **39%**

Everyday expenses **27%**

Paying down debt **43%**

Vacation **13%**

Major purchase **11%**

Note: Multiple responses allowed.

Source: National Retail Federation 2007 Tax Returns Consumer Intentions and Actions survey of 9,027 consumers conducted by BIGresearch. Margin of error ±1 percentage point.

By Jae Yang and Veronica Salazar, USA TODAY

USA TODAY Snapshots®

Falling for clothes shopping

What adults plan to spend most on this fall:

Clothing **57%**

School supplies **15%**

Home decor **14%**

Home office supplies **6%**

Don't know **8%**

Source: Opinion Research Corporation telephone survey for Discover Card of 1,031 adults, July 14–17. Margin of error: ±3 percentage points.

By Mary Cadden and Karl Gelles, USA TODAY

■ Saving

If you had $100,000 to invest, would you put it in mutual funds? The stock market? Bonds? Would you invest in real estate? Deposit it into your checking account? Or would you do none of the above and buy that sports car or that Birkin bag you've been eyeing? What would your financial advisor do with the same sum of cash?

How many of us expect to work after we retire? How much money do you think you need in order to retire comfortably? Is that above or below the average estimate? Are you adverse to risk when it comes to investing? Do men or women tend to take more risks in the stock market? Would it surprise you to know that the majority of investors look at a company's track record for social responsibility? What is your biggest investment mistake?

Are you ready for your close-up?

USA TODAY Snapshots®

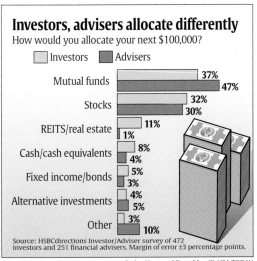

Investors, advisers allocate differently

How would you allocate your next $100,000?

Investors ▪ Advisers

Mutual funds	37% / 47%
Stocks	32% / 30%
REITS/real estate	11% / 1%
Cash/cash equivalents	8% / 4%
Fixed income/bonds	5% / 3%
Alternative investments	4% / 5%
Other	3% / 10%

Source: HSBCdirections Investor/Adviser survey of 472 investors and 251 financial advisers. Margin of error ±3 percentage points.

By Jae Yang and Dave Merrill, USA TODAY

USA TODAY Snapshots®

Investment mistakes

What is your biggest investment mistake?

Investing too much in one company/sector
13%

Not pulling out of poorly performing investments
10%

Getting rid of investments too quickly
8%

Not contributing enough to retirement funds
8%

Being too conservative
6%

Source: Citigroup Smith Barney's Affluent Investor survey of 585 investors with $100,000 or more in financial assets. Margin of error ±4 percentage points.

By Jae Yang and Alejandro Gonzalez, USA TODAY

USA TODAY Snapshots®

Women are more risk averse in stock market

If both the stock market and a stock you owned dropped 25% in three months, what would you do?

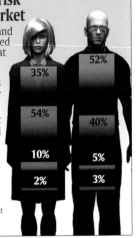

Buy more shares while the price is low

35% | 52%

Hold shares and wait for a turnaround

54% | 40%

Sell some of shares

10% | 5%

Sell all shares

2% | 3%

Source: ShareBuilder Women and Investing survey of 965 women and 1,066 men 18 and older. Margin of error ±3 percentage points.

By Jae Yang and Bob Laird, USA TODAY

USA TODAY Snapshots®

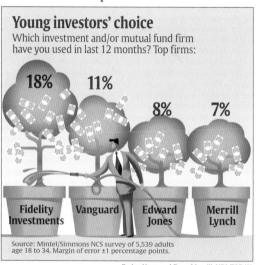

Young investors' choice
Which investment and/or mutual fund firm
have you used in last 12 months? Top firms:

18%   11%

8%   7%

Fidelity   Vanguard   Edward   Merrill
Investments   Jones   Lynch

Source: Mintel/Simmons NCS survey of 5,539 adults
age 18 to 34. Margin of error ±1 percentage points.

By Jae Yang and Dave Merrill, USA TODAY

USA TODAY Snapshots®

Socially responsible investing

Seventy percent of respondents check a company's track record on socially responsible issues. Have you changed an investment decision because of a company's poor performance on social issues?

Source: Yankelovich OmniPlus Monitor survey of 600 investors. Margin of error: ±4 percentage points.

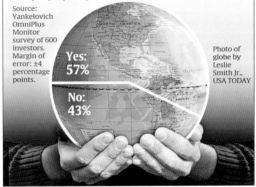

Yes: 57%

No: 43%

Photo of globe by Leslie Smith Jr., USA TODAY

By Jae Yang and Karl Gelles, USA TODAY

USA TODAY Snapshots®

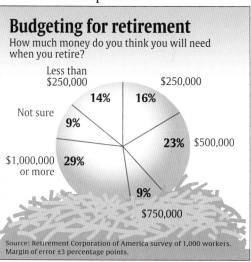

Budgeting for retirement

How much money do you think you will need when you retire?

Less than $250,000 — **14%**

$250,000 — **16%**

Not sure — **9%**

$500,000 — **23%**

$1,000,000 or more — **29%**

$750,000 — **9%**

Source: Retirement Corporation of America survey of 1,000 workers.
Margin of error ±3 percentage points.

By Jae Yang and Sam Ward, USA TODAY

USA TODAY Snapshots®

Debt in retirement

About one in three 62- to 75-year-olds surveyed have or expect to have debt after retirement. Major sources of debt in retirement:

Credit cards **58%**

Mortgage **52%**

Auto loan **39%**

Home repairs maintenance **29%**

Health care costs **28%**

Note: Multiple responses allowed

Source: Financial Freedom survey of 1,129 retired and pre-retired adults age 62 to 75. Margin of error ±3 percentage points.

By Jae Yang and Alejandro Gonzalez, USA TODAY

USA TODAY Snapshots®

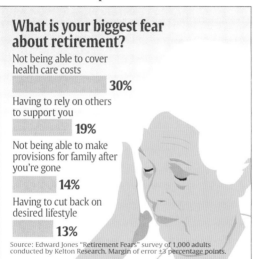

What is your biggest fear about retirement?

Not being able to cover health care costs

30%

Having to rely on others to support you

19%

Not being able to make provisions for family after you're gone

14%

Having to cut back on desired lifestyle

13%

Source: Edward Jones "Retirement Fears" survey of 1,000 adults conducted by Kelton Research. Margin of error ±3 percentage points.

By Jae Yang and Keith Simmons, USA TODAY

USA TODAY Snapshots®

Many plan to work after retirement

What income sources other than Social Security do you expect to have during your retirement years? Top sources:

Savings and investments such as a 401(k) and stocks
52%

Employment
43%

Employer pension
39%

Individual retirement account
36%

Inheritance
16%

Note: Multiple responses allowed
Source: Thrivent Financial Retirement survey of 2,500 adults 45 to 64 years old conducted by Action Marketing Research. Margin of error ±2 percentage points.

By Jae Yang and Bob Laird, USA TODAY

USA TODAY Snapshots®

More crimes, same money

Although state court prosecutors reported they faced more complex cases and issues in 2005 than in previous years—such as computer crime and identity theft—the budget has barely changed. Median annual budget for state prosecutors' offices (in thousands):

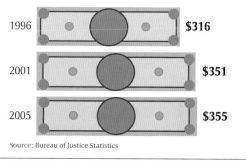

1996   **$316**

2001   **$351**

2005   **$355**

Source: Bureau of Justice Statistics

By David Stuckey and Adrienne Lewis, USA TODAY

USA TODAY Snapshots®

Emergency fund

63% of respondents say they have an emergency fund in case of a major expense. How long would it last?

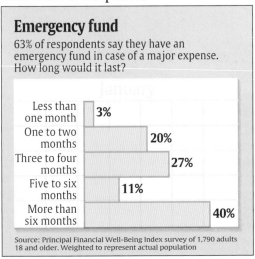

Less than one month	**3%**
One to two months	**20%**
Three to four months	**27%**
Five to six months	**11%**
More than six months	**40%**

Source: Principal Financial Well-Being Index survey of 1,790 adults 18 and older. Weighted to represent actual population

By Jae Yang and Adrienne Lewis, USA TODAY

USA TODAY Snapshots®

Keeping schools running

Average hourly wages for selected school workers:

$14.18 — Bus drivers

$12.61 — Custodians

$10.33 — Cafeteria workers

Source: Census Bureau

By David Stuckey and Julie Snider, USA TODAY

USA TODAY Snapshots®

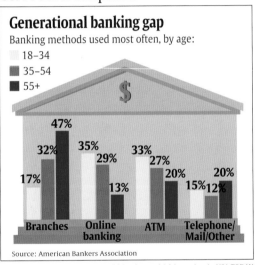

Generational banking gap

Banking methods used most often, by age:

- 18–34
- 35–54
- 55+

	Branches	Online banking	ATM	Telephone/Mail/Other
18–34	17%	35%	33%	15%
35–54	32%	29%	27%	12%
55+	47%	13%	20%	20%

Source: American Bankers Association

By David Stuckey and Adrienne Lewis, USA TODAY

USA TODAY Snapshots®

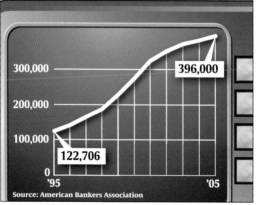

More chances to bank

From 1995 to 2005, the number of ATM machines in the USA tripled:

396,000

122,706

'95   '05

Source: American Bankers Association

By David Stuckey and Julie Snider, USA TODAY

USA TODAY Snapshots®

New news sources

Percentage of people in each age group saying they get at least some of their news from cellphones, PDAs and/or podcasts:

Age

18–29   **13%**

30–49   **10%**

50–64   **3%**

65–plus   **1%**

Source: Pew Research Center for the People and the Press.

By Sam Ward, USA TODAY

USA TODAY Snapshots®

How would you expand your portfolio into a foreign market?

Invest in a mutual fund with exposure to that market **29%**

Invest in an exchange-traded fund with exposure to that market **26%**

Purchase American depositary receipts in the U.S. market **16%**

Increase ownership in a U.S. company doing business in foreign markets **11%**

Source: TD Ameritrade survey of 561 investors. Margin of error ±5 percentage points.

By Jae Yang and Dave Merrill, USA TODAY

USA TODAY Snapshots®

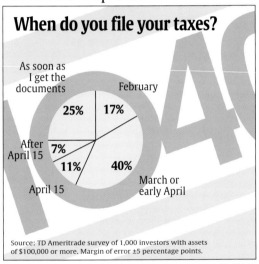

When do you file your taxes?

As soon as I get the documents
25%

February
17%

After April 15
7%

11%
April 15

40%
March or early April

Source: TD Ameritrade survey of 1,000 investors with assets of $100,000 or more. Margin of error ±5 percentage points.

By Jae Yang and Sam Ward, USA TODAY

USA TODAY Snapshots®

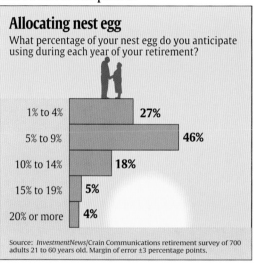

Allocating nest egg

What percentage of your nest egg do you anticipate using during each year of your retirement?

1% to 4%	**27%**
5% to 9%	**46%**
10% to 14%	**18%**
15% to 19%	**5%**
20% or more	**4%**

Source: *InvestmentNews*/Crain Communications retirement survey of 700 adults 21 to 60 years old. Margin of error ±3 percentage points.

By Jae Yang and Adrienne Lewis, USA TODAY

USA TODAY Snapshots®

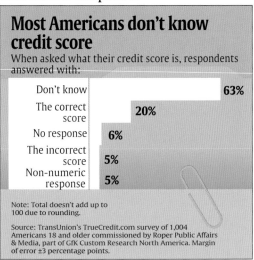

Most Americans don't know credit score

When asked what their credit score is, respondents answered with:

Don't know	63%
The correct score	20%
No response	6%
The incorrect score	5%
Non-numeric response	5%

Note: Total doesn't add up to 100 due to rounding.

Source: TransUnion's TrueCredit.com survey of 1,004 Americans 18 and older commissioned by Roper Public Affairs & Media, part of GfK Custom Research North America. Margin of error ±3 percentage points.

By Jae Yang and Adrienne Lewis, USA TODAY

USA TODAY Snapshots®

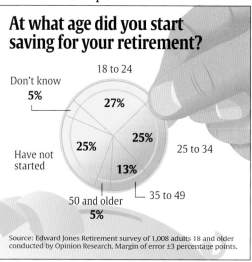

At what age did you start saving for your retirement?

18 to 24

Don't know
5%

27%

25%

25 to 34

Have not started

25%

13%

35 to 49

50 and older

5%

Source: Edward Jones Retirement survey of 1,008 adults 18 and older conducted by Opinion Research. Margin of error ±3 percentage points.

By Jae Yang and Veronica Salazar, USA TODAY

USA TODAY Snapshots®

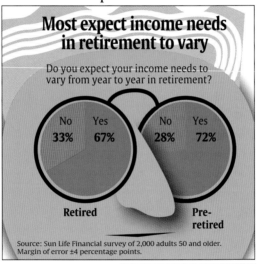

Most expect income needs in retirement to vary

Do you expect your income needs to vary from year to year in retirement?

No	Yes
33%	67%

Retired

No	Yes
28%	72%

Pre-retired

Source: Sun Life Financial survey of 2,000 adults 50 and older. Margin of error ±4 percentage points.

By Jae Yang and Julie Snider, USA TODAY

USA TODAY Snapshots®

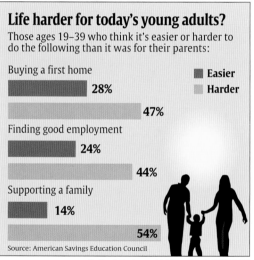

Life harder for today's young adults?

Those ages 19–39 who think it's easier or harder to do the following than it was for their parents:

Buying a first home

■ **Easier**
■ **Harder**

28%

47%

Finding good employment

24%

44%

Supporting a family

14%

54%

Source: American Savings Education Council

By David Stuckey and Adrienne Lewis, USA TODAY

USA TODAY Snapshots®

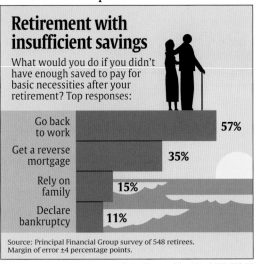

Retirement with insufficient savings

What would you do if you didn't have enough saved to pay for basic necessities after your retirement? Top responses:

Go back to work — 57%
Get a reverse mortgage — 35%
Rely on family — 15%
Declare bankruptcy — 11%

Source: Principal Financial Group survey of 548 retirees. Margin of error ±4 percentage points.

By Jae Yang and Sam Ward, USA TODAY

106

USA TODAY Snapshots®

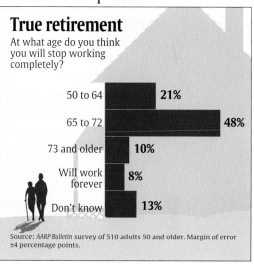

True retirement

At what age do you think
you will stop working
completely?

- 50 to 64 — **21%**
- 65 to 72 — **48%**
- 73 and older — **10%**
- Will work forever — **8%**
- Don't know — **13%**

Source: *AARP Bulletin* survey of 510 adults 50 and older. Margin of error ±4 percentage points.

By Jae Yang and Robert W. Ahrens, USA TODAY

USA TODAY Snapshots®

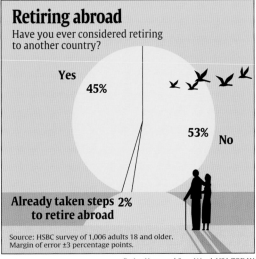

Retiring abroad

Have you ever considered retiring
to another country?

Yes
45%

53% No

Already taken steps **2%**
to retire abroad

Source: HSBC survey of 1,006 adults 18 and older.
Margin of error ±3 percentage points.

By Jae Yang and Sam Ward, USA TODAY

USA TODAY Snapshots®

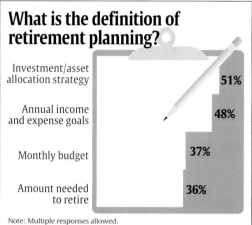

What is the definition of retirement planning?

Investment/asset allocation strategy **51%**

Annual income and expense goals **48%**

Monthly budget **37%**

Amount needed to retire **36%**

Note: Multiple responses allowed.
Source: Bank Administration Institute and Mercatus survey of 2,997 consumers age 35 to 70 with investable assets of $50,000 to $2 million.
Margin of error ±2 percentage points.

By Jae Yang and Adrienne Lewis, USA TODAY

USA TODAY Snapshots®

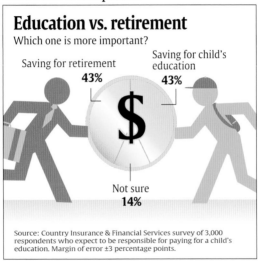

Education vs. retirement

Which one is more important?

Saving for retirement
43%

Saving for child's education
43%

Not sure
14%

Source: Country Insurance & Financial Services survey of 3,000 respondents who expect to be responsible for paying for a child's education. Margin of error ±3 percentage points.

By Jae Yang and Veronica Salazar, USA TODAY

USA TODAY Snapshots®

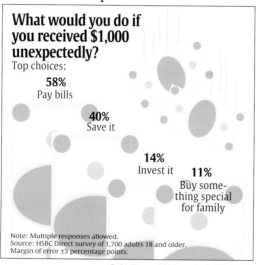

What would you do if you received $1,000 unexpectedly?

Top choices:

58%
Pay bills

40%
Save it

14%
Invest it

11%
Buy something special for family

Note: Multiple responses allowed.
Source: HSBC Direct survey of 1,700 adults 18 and older.
Margin of error ±3 percentage points.

By Jae Yang and Adrienne Lewis, USA TODAY

USA TODAY Snapshots®

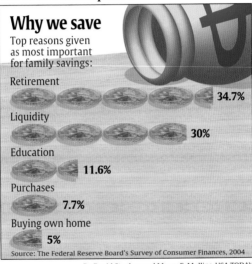

Why we save

Top reasons given as most important for family savings:

Retirement
34.7%

Liquidity
30%

Education
11.6%

Purchases
7.7%

Buying own home
5%

Source: The Federal Reserve Board's Survey of Consumer Finances, 2004

By David Stuckey and Marcy E. Mullins, USA TODAY

USA TODAY Snapshots®

Pay raise may not match cost-of-living rise

Social Security benefits rose by 3.3% in 2007 to account for an increase in the cost of living. Did or will your most recent pay raise cover the increase?

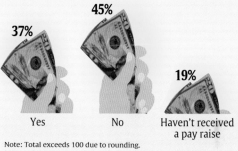

37%
Yes

45%
No

19%
Haven't received a pay raise

Note: Total exceeds 100 due to rounding.
Source: American Payroll Association 2007 "Getting Paid in America" survey of 47,192 workers. Margin of error ±1 percentage points.

By Jae Yang and Alejandro Gonzalez, USA TODAY

USA TODAY Snapshots®

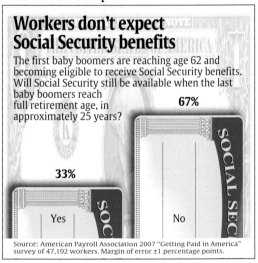

Workers don't expect Social Security benefits

The first baby boomers are reaching age 62 and becoming eligible to receive Social Security benefits. Will Social Security still be available when the last baby boomers reach full retirement age, in approximately 25 years?

67%

33%

Yes

No

Source: American Payroll Association 2007 "Getting Paid in America" survey of 47,192 workers. Margin of error ±1 percentage points.

By Jae Yang and Marcy E. Mullins, USA TODAY

USA TODAY Snapshots®

Women more concerned about investing in stock market

What is your biggest concern with investing in the stock market? Top concerns:

Women   Men

Risk — 25% (Women), 20% (Men)

Not understanding the market language — 23% (Women), 10% (Men)

Not having enough time to invest — 14% (Women), 18% (Men)

Source: ShareBuilder survey of 2,033 adults 21 and older.
Margin of error: ±2 percentage points.

By Jae Yang and Karl Gelles, USA TODAY

USA TODAY Snapshots®

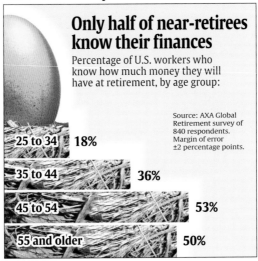

Only half of near-retirees know their finances

Percentage of U.S. workers who know how much money they will have at retirement, by age group:

Source: AXA Global Retirement survey of 840 respondents. Margin of error ±2 percentage points.

Age group	Percentage
25 to 34	18%
35 to 44	36%
45 to 54	53%
55 and older	50%

By Jae Yang and Karl Gelles, USA TODAY

116

USA TODAY Snapshots®

Saving for vacation

How long do you save up to pay for a vacation that is at least a week long?

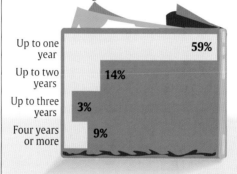

Up to one year — 59%

Up to two years — 14%

Up to three years — 3%

Four years or more — 9%

Source: Capital One Direct Banking survey of 1,008 adults 18 and older. Margin of error ±3 percentage points.

By Jae Yang and Robert W. Ahrens, USA TODAY

Did you know that by the time we turn thirty-five, almost 80 percent of us are married or have been married? Of that 80 percent, how many will admit to missing aspects of the single life? Would you? What would you say you miss most? What would your spouse say?

Those who are still dating, what are you looking for in your mate? What keeps you from returning his or her calls? Would you be more turned off if your first date had poor table manners, bad breath, or frumpy clothes? Is body odor a deal breaker? How many people meet their significant others at work? How many meet through friends? Or the Internet? How long is normal for waiting to get engaged? Would the size of the rock matter to you?

Where do you stand?

USA TODAY Snapshots®

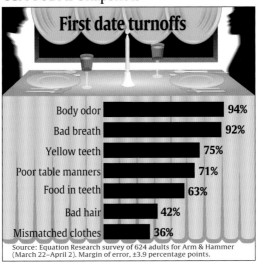

First date turnoffs

Body odor	94%
Bad breath	92%
Yellow teeth	75%
Poor table manners	71%
Food in teeth	63%
Bad hair	42%
Mismatched clothes	36%

Source: Equation Research survey of 624 adults for Arm & Hammer (March 22–April 2). Margin of error, ±3.9 percentage points.

By Mary Cadden and Marcy E. Mullins, USA TODAY

USA TODAY Snapshots®

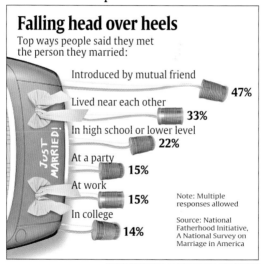

Falling head over heels

Top ways people said they met
the person they married:

Introduced by mutual friend — **47%**

Lived near each other — **33%**

In high school or lower level — **22%**

At a party — **15%**

At work — **15%**

In college — **14%**

Note: Multiple
responses allowed

Source: National
Fatherhood Initiative,
A National Survey on
Marriage in America

By David Stuckey and Karl Gelles, USA TODAY

USA TODAY Snapshots®

Romance at work

Did you meet your significant other at work?

Yes
38%

No
62%

Source: Yahoo HotJobs survey of 11,908 workers. Margin of error ±3 percentage points.

By Jae Yang and Sam Ward, USA TODAY

USA TODAY Snapshots®

All work, no play

Does your workplace have a policy against romances between co-workers?

Yes **33%**

No **45%**

Don't know **22%**

Source:
Yahoo HotJobs survey of 7,184 workers.
Margin of error ±3 percentage points.

By Jae Yang and Sam Ward, USA TODAY

USA TODAY Snapshots®

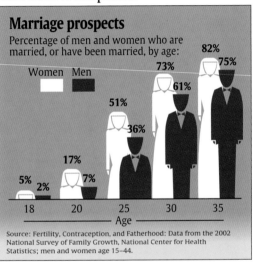

Marriage prospects

Percentage of men and women who are married, or have been married, by age:

Women   Men

Age	Women	Men
18	5%	2%
20	17%	7%
25	51%	36%
30	73%	61%
35	82%	75%

Source: Fertility, Contraception, and Fatherhood: Data from the 2002 National Survey of Family Growth, National Center for Health Statistics; men and women age 15–44.

By Tracey Wong Briggs and Sam Ward, USA TODAY

USA TODAY Snapshots®

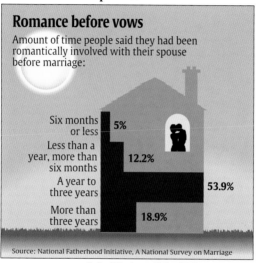

Romance before vows

Amount of time people said they had been romantically involved with their spouse before marriage:

Six months or less — 5%

Less than a year, more than six months — 12.2%

A year to three years — 53.9%

More than three years — 18.9%

Source: National Fatherhood Initiative, A National Survey on Marriage

By David Stuckey and Robert W. Ahrens, USA TODAY

USA TODAY Snapshots®

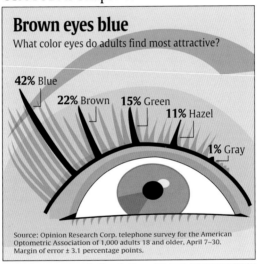

Brown eyes blue
What color eyes do adults find most attractive?

42% Blue

22% Brown   **15%** Green

11% Hazel

1% Gray

Source: Opinion Research Corp. telephone survey for the American Optometric Association of 1,000 adults 18 and older, April 7–30. Margin of error ± 3.1 percentage points.

By Mary Cadden and Veronica Salazar, USA TODAY

USA TODAY Snapshots®

Finding a long-lost love
The best way to contact him or her[1]:

E-mail **32%**

Face to face **23%**

Telephone **23%**

Letter **19%**

Other **4%**

1 – Does not equal 100% due to rounding.

Source: Harris Interactive survey for
WhitePages.com of 2,395 adults from Jan. 3–5.
Margin of error ±3 percentage points.

By Mary Cadden and Veronica Salazar, USA TODAY

USA TODAY Snapshots®

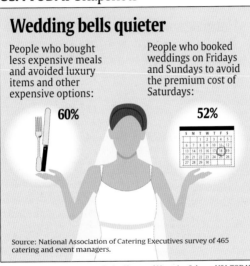

Wedding bells quieter

People who bought less expensive meals and avoided luxury items and other expensive options:

60%

People who booked weddings on Fridays and Sundays to avoid the premium cost of Saturdays:

52%

Source: National Association of Catering Executives survey of 465 catering and event managers.

By Jae Yang and Veronica Salazar, USA TODAY

USA TODAY Snapshots®

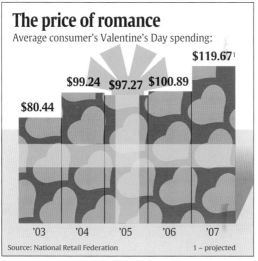

The price of romance

Average consumer's Valentine's Day spending:

$80.44 — '03
$99.24 — '04
$97.27 — '05
$100.89 — '06
$119.67[1] — '07

Source: National Retail Federation   1 – projected

By David Stuckey and Sam Ward, USA TODAY

USA TODAY Snapshots®

Proposing with a ring?

The average cost of a diamond engagement ring in 2006 was $3,210. The most popular diamond shapes for engagement rings:

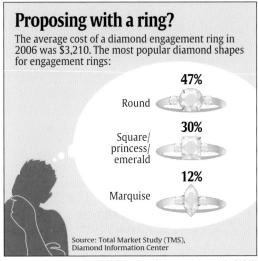

47%
Round

30%
Square/princess/emerald

12%
Marquise

Source: Total Market Study (TMS), Diamond Information Center

By Michelle Healy and Veronica Salazar, USA TODAY

USA TODAY Snapshots®

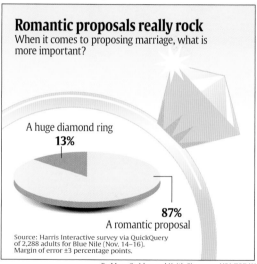

Romantic proposals really rock
When it comes to proposing marriage, what is more important?

A huge diamond ring
13%

87%
A romantic proposal

Source: Harris Interactive survey via QuickQuery of 2,288 adults for Blue Nile (Nov. 14–16). Margin of error ±3 percentage points.

By Mary Cadden and Keith Simmons, USA TODAY

USA TODAY Snapshots®

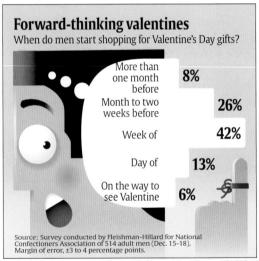

Forward-thinking valentines
When do men start shopping for Valentine's Day gifts?

More than one month before	8%
Month to two weeks before	26%
Week of	42%
Day of	13%
On the way to see Valentine	6%

Source: Survey conducted by Fleishman-Hillard for National Confectioners Association of 514 adult men (Dec. 15-18). Margin of error, ±3 to 4 percentage points.

By Mary Cadden and Frank Pompa, USA TODAY

USA TODAY Snapshots®

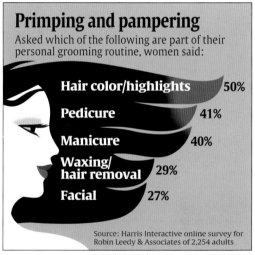

Primping and pampering

Asked which of the following are part of their personal grooming routine, women said:

Hair color/highlights — 50%

Pedicure — 41%

Manicure — 40%

Waxing/hair removal — 29%

Facial — 27%

Source: Harris Interactive online survey for Robin Leedy & Associates of 2,254 adults

By Michelle Healy and Sam Ward, USA TODAY

USA TODAY Snapshots®

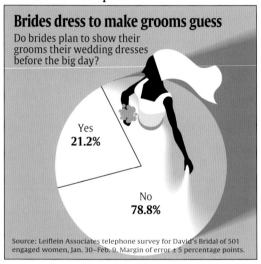

Brides dress to make grooms guess

Do brides plan to show their grooms their wedding dresses before the big day?

Yes
21.2%

No
78.8%

Source: Leiflein Associates telephone survey for David's Bridal of 501 engaged women, Jan. 30–Feb. 9. Margin of error ± 5 percentage points.

By Mary Cadden and Sam Ward, USA TODAY

USA TODAY Snapshots®

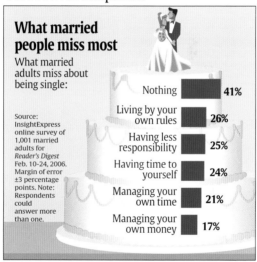

What married people miss most

What married adults miss about being single:

Source: InsightExpress online survey of 1,001 married adults for *Reader's Digest* Feb. 10-24, 2006. Margin of error ±3 percentage points. Note: Respondents could answer more than one.

Nothing **41%**

Living by your own rules **26%**

Having less responsibility **25%**

Having time to yourself **24%**

Managing your own time **21%**

Managing your own money **17%**

By Mary Cadden and Dave Merrill, USA TODAY

USA TODAY Snapshots®

Marriage counseling a law?

Percentage of people who agree or disagree that couples considering marriage should be required by law to have premarital counseling:

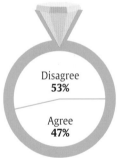

Disagree
53%

Agree
47%

Source: National Fatherhood Initiative, A National Survey on Marriage in America of 1,503 adults in 2003-04. Margin of error ±3 percentage points.

By David Stuckey and Adrienne Lewis, USA TODAY

USA TODAY Snapshots®

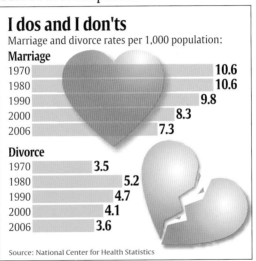

I dos and I don'ts

Marriage and divorce rates per 1,000 population:

Marriage

Year	Rate
1970	10.6
1980	10.6
1990	9.8
2000	8.3
2006	7.3

Divorce

Year	Rate
1970	3.5
1980	5.2
1990	4.7
2000	4.1
2006	3.6

Source: National Center for Health Statistics

By David Stuckey and Alejandro Gonzalez, USA TODAY

USA TODAY Snapshots®

Love blooms

Whom women buy flowers for on Valentine's Day:

Mother	**32%**
Husband/ significant other	**24%**
Self	**22%**

Source: IPSOS FloralTrends, 2005

By David Stuckey and Julie Snider, USA TODAY

USA TODAY Snapshots®

International love

Number of foreign nationals who came to the USA to marry an American using a "fiancé(e) visa":

Year	Number
1990	6,545
1995	7,793
2000	20,558
2004	28,546

Source: Department of Homeland Security

By David Stuckey and Karl Gelles, USA TODAY

USA TODAY Snapshots®

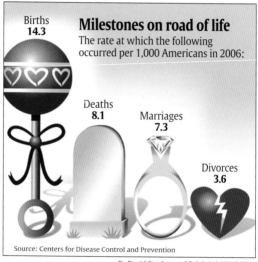

Milestones on road of life

The rate at which the following occurred per 1,000 Americans in 2006:

Births
14.3

Deaths
8.1

Marriages
7.3

Divorces
3.6

Source: Centers for Disease Control and Prevention

By David Stuckey and Bob Laird, USA TODAY

USA TODAY Snapshots®

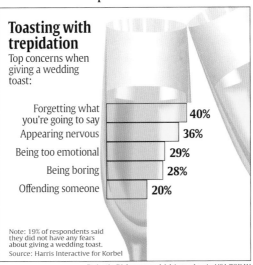

Toasting with trepidation

Top concerns when giving a wedding toast:

Forgetting what you're going to say	**40%**
Appearing nervous	**36%**
Being too emotional	**29%**
Being boring	**28%**
Offending someone	**20%**

Note: 19% of respondents said they did not have any fears about giving a wedding toast.
Source: Harris Interactive for Korbel

By Justin Dickerson and Adrienne Lewis, USA TODAY

How many nights each week do you sit down to eat with your family? Is that more or fewer nights than others do? What sorts of rules do you put in place for your children? Do you limit their time in front of the television? Do you restrict their activities online? How many parents do?

How many hours do other moms spend cleaning? How many dads are stay-at-home dads? What kind of non-parental child care is most commonly employed? How many times a month are adults in touch with their parents by phone? How many times a day do you tell your children you love them? Is it more common to express affection when they're under the age of six than when they're older?

How do you stack up?

USA TODAY Snapshots®

Where we live in relation to our moms

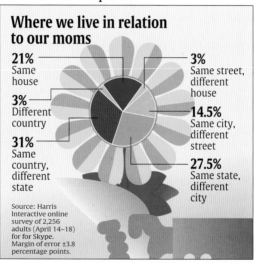

21%
Same house

3%
Different country

31%
Same country, different state

3%
Same street, different house

14.5%
Same city, different street

27.5%
Same state, different city

Source: Harris Interactive online survey of 2,256 adults (April 14–18) for for Skype. Margin of error ±3.8 percentage points.

By Mary Cadden and Alejandro Gonzalez, USA TODAY

USA TODAY Snapshots®

Support from the folks
Percentage of children who are praised at least three times per day by their mom or dad:

72%   51%   37%

Under 6   6–11   12–17

Source: Census Bureau's "A Child's Day" report

By Alejandro Gonzalez, USA TODAY

USA TODAY Snapshots®

Frequency of family meals

How often we eat at home as a family during the week:

Once a week	2%
2 times	6%
3 times	7%
4 times	7%
5 times	24%
6 times	23%
7 or more	28%
Never	2%

Note: Percentages do not equal 100 due to rounding

Source: Harris Interactive online survey for SuperTarget of 496 adults living with children under 18, March 23–27. Margin of error ±6.5 percentage points.

By Mary Cadden and Marcy E. Mullins, USA TODAY

USA TODAY Snapshots®

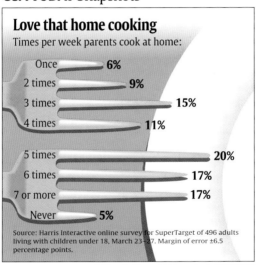

Love that home cooking

Times per week parents cook at home:

Once — **6%**

2 times — **9%**

3 times — **15%**

4 times — **11%**

5 times — **20%**

6 times — **17%**

7 or more — **17%**

Never — **5%**

Source: Harris Interactive online survey for SuperTarget of 496 adults living with children under 18, March 23–27. Margin of error ±6.5 percentage points.

By Mary Cadden and Adrienne Lewis, USA TODAY

USA TODAY Snapshots®

The importance of fatherhood

Percentage of fathers who agreed with these statements about fatherhood:

91%

There is a father-absence crisis in the USA.

81%

Men perform better as fathers when they are married to the mothers of their children.

67%

The government should do more to help and support fathers.

Source: National Fatherhood Initiative

By David Stuckey and Marcy E. Mullins, USA TODAY

USA TODAY Snapshots®

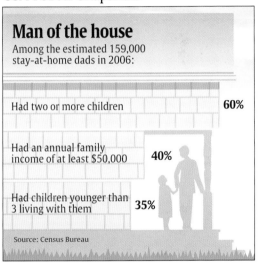

Man of the house

Among the estimated 159,000 stay-at-home dads in 2006:

Had two or more children — **60%**

Had an annual family income of at least $50,000 — **40%**

Had children younger than 3 living with them — **35%**

Source: Census Bureau

By David Stuckey and Karl Gelles, USA TODAY

USA TODAY Snapshots®

Moms clock cleanup time

How many hours a week mothers spend cleaning the house:

1–5 hours	61%
6–10 hours	23%
11–15 hours	7%
16–20 hours	3%
More than 21 hours	5%
None	2%

Note: Does not equal 100 due to rounding

Source: Harris Interactive survey for Edelman of 801 mothers, March 8–13. Margin of error ±5 percentage points

By Mary Cadden and Karl Gelles, USA TODAY

USA TODAY Snapshots®

Some moms too tired to drive
Percentage of mothers who ...

31%

19%

11%

Admit to driving while drowsy at least once a month

Have driven drowsy with kids in the car

Are likely to take a nap when tired

Source: National Sleep Foundation

By David Stuckey and Marcy E. Mullins, USA TODAY

USA TODAY Snapshots®

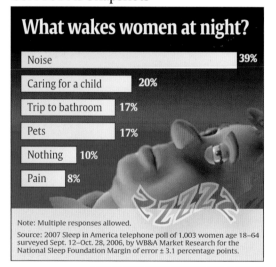

What wakes women at night?

Noise	39%
Caring for a child	20%
Trip to bathroom	17%
Pets	17%
Nothing	10%
Pain	8%

Note: Multiple responses allowed.

Source: 2007 Sleep in America telephone poll of 1,003 women age 18–64 surveyed Sept. 12–Oct. 28, 2006, by WB&A Market Research for the National Sleep Foundation Margin of error ± 3.1 percentage points.

By Tracey Wong Briggs and Suzy Parker, USA TODAY

USA TODAY Snapshots®

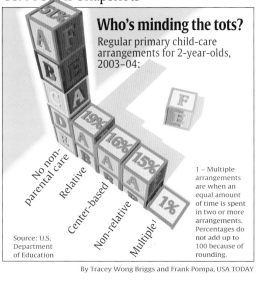

Who's minding the tots?

Regular primary child-care arrangements for 2-year-olds, 2003–04:

No non-parental care — 19%

Relative — 16%

Center-based — 15%

Non-relative —

Multiple¹ — 1%

1 – Multiple arrangements are when an equal amount of time is spent in two or more arrangements. Percentages do not add up to 100 because of rounding.

Source: U.S. Department of Education

By Tracey Wong Briggs and Frank Pompa, USA TODAY

USA TODAY Snapshots®

Aging drivers steer family concerns

Most difficult topic to discuss with elderly parents:

No answer **2%**

36% Stop driving

Other **15%**

18%

29%

Funeral wishes

Selling their house

Source: National Safety Council/caring.com survey of 1,011 adults ages 44–62 with parents age 65 or older conducted online by Knowledge Networks April 15–21, 2008.

By Anne R. Carey and Suzy Parker, USA TODAY

USA TODAY Snapshots®

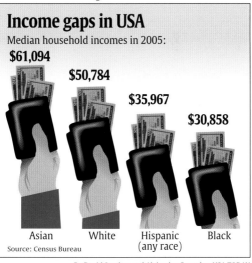

Income gaps in USA

Median household incomes in 2005:

$61,094 — Asian

$50,784 — White

$35,967 — Hispanic (any race)

$30,858 — Black

Source: Census Bureau

By David Stuckey and Alejandro Gonzalez, USA TODAY

USA TODAY Snapshots®

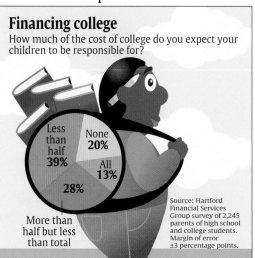

Financing college
How much of the cost of college do you expect your children to be responsible for?

Less than half **39%**

None **20%**

All **13%**

28%

More than half but less than total

Source: Hartford Financial Services Group survey of 2,245 parents of high school and college students. Margin of error ±3 percentage points.

By Jae Yang and Alejandro Gonzalez, USA TODAY

USA TODAY Snapshots®

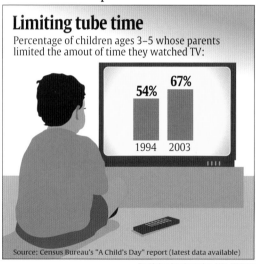

Limiting tube time

Percentage of children ages 3–5 whose parents limited the amout of time they watched TV:

54% 1994

67% 2003

Source: Census Bureau's "A Child's Day" report (latest data available)

By Alejandro Gonzalez, USA TODAY

USA TODAY Snapshots®

Read me a story

Percentage of children ages 3–5 who were read to every day in the previous week by a family member, in selected years:

52.8%   58.0%   56.5%   53.5%   57.5%   60.3%

'93   '95   '96   '99   '01   '05

Source: Department of Education

By David Stuckey and Sam Ward, USA TODAY

USA TODAY Snapshots®

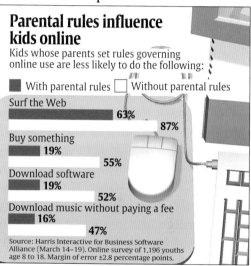

Parental rules influence kids online

Kids whose parents set rules governing online use are less likely to do the following:

■ With parental rules ☐ Without parental rules

Surf the Web
63%
87%

Buy something
19%
55%

Download software
19%
52%

Download music without paying a fee
16%
47%

Source: Harris Interactive for Business Software Alliance (March 14–19). Online survey of 1,196 youths age 8 to 18. Margin of error ±2.8 percentage points.

By Cindy Clark and Karl Gelles, USA TODAY

USA TODAY Snapshots®

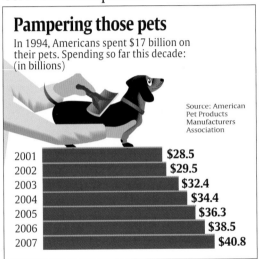

Pampering those pets

In 1994, Americans spent $17 billion on their pets. Spending so far this decade: (in billions)

Source: American Pet Products Manufacturers Association

Year	Spending
2001	$28.5
2002	$29.5
2003	$32.4
2004	$34.4
2005	$36.3
2006	$38.5
2007	$40.8

By Karl Gelles, USA TODAY

160

USA TODAY Snapshots®

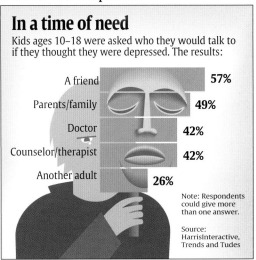

In a time of need

Kids ages 10–18 were asked who they would talk to if they thought they were depressed. The results:

A friend — **57%**

Parents/family — **49%**

Doctor — **42%**

Counselor/therapist — **42%**

Another adult — **26%**

Note: Respondents could give more than one answer.

Source: HarrisInteractive, Trends and Tudes

By David Stuckey and Karl Gelles, USA TODAY

USA TODAY Snapshots®

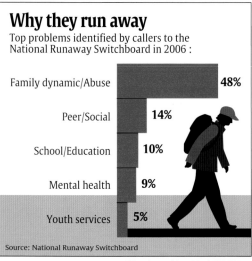

Why they run away

Top problems identified by callers to the
National Runaway Switchboard in 2006 :

Family dynamic/Abuse — 48%

Peer/Social — 14%

School/Education — 10%

Mental health — 9%

Youth services — 5%

Source: National Runaway Switchboard

By David Stuckey and Sam Ward, USA TODAY

USA TODAY Snapshots®

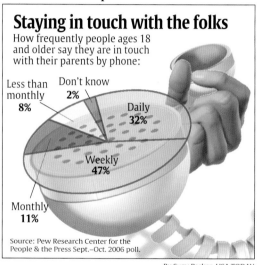

Staying in touch with the folks

How frequently people ages 18 and older say they are in touch with their parents by phone:

Less than monthly
8%

Don't know
2%

Daily
32%

Weekly
47%

Monthly
11%

Source: Pew Research Center for the People & the Press Sept.–Oct. 2006 poll.

By Suzy Parker, USA TODAY

USA TODAY Snapshots®

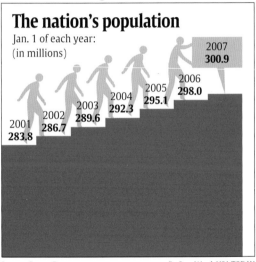

The nation's population

Jan. 1 of each year:
(in millions)

2001 **283.8**

2002 **286.7**

2003 **289.6**

2004 **292.3**

2005 **295.1**

2006 **298.0**

2007 **300.9**

Source: Census Bureau   By Sam Ward, USA TODAY

USA TODAY Snapshots®

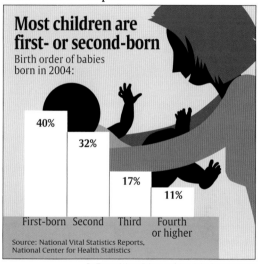

Most children are first- or second-born

Birth order of babies born in 2004:

- 40% First-born
- 32% Second
- 17% Third
- 11% Fourth or higher

Source: National Vital Statistics Reports, National Center for Health Statistics

By Tracey Wong Briggs and Sam Ward, USA TODAY

USA TODAY Snapshots®

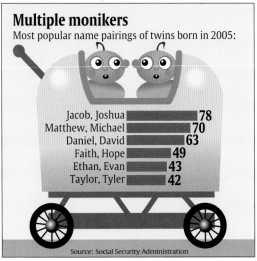

Multiple monikers
Most popular name pairings of twins born in 2005:

Name pairing	Count
Jacob, Joshua	78
Matthew, Michael	70
Daniel, David	63
Faith, Hope	49
Ethan, Evan	43
Taylor, Tyler	42

Source: Social Security Administration

By Tracey Wong Briggs and Alejandro Gonzalez, USA TODAY

USA TODAY Snapshots®

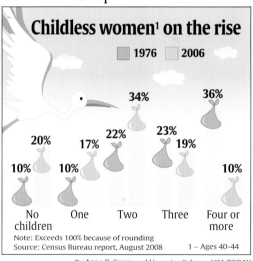

Childless women[1] on the rise

■ 1976 ☐ 2006

No children
- 10%
- 20%

One
- 10%
- 17%

Two
- 22%
- 34%

Three
- 23%
- 19%

Four or more
- 36%
- 10%

Note: Exceeds 100% because of rounding
Source: Census Bureau report, August 2008

1 – Ages 40-44

By Anne R. Carey and Veronica Salazar, USA TODAY

USA TODAY Snapshots®

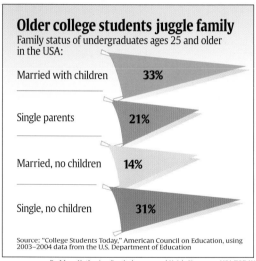

Older college students juggle family

Family status of undergraduates ages 25 and older in the USA:

Married with children — **33%**

Single parents — **21%**

Married, no children — **14%**

Single, no children — **31%**

Source: "College Students Today," American Council on Education, using 2003–2004 data from the U.S. Department of Education

By Mary Katherine Bartholomew and Keith Simmons, USA TODAY

USA TODAY Snapshots®

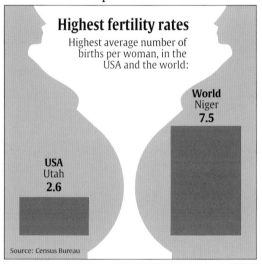

Highest fertility rates

Highest average number of
births per woman, in the
USA and the world:

World
Niger
7.5

USA
Utah
2.6

Source: Census Bureau

By David Stuckey and Sam Ward, USA TODAY

USA TODAY Snapshots®

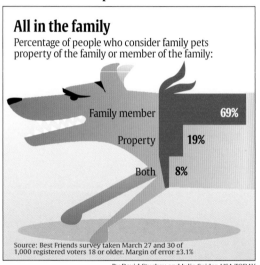

All in the family

Percentage of people who consider family pets property of the family or member of the family:

Family member **69%**

Property **19%**

Both **8%**

Source: Best Friends survey taken March 27 and 30 of 1,000 registered voters 18 or older. Margin of error ±3.1%

By David Stuckey and Julie Snider, USA TODAY

USA TODAY Snapshots®

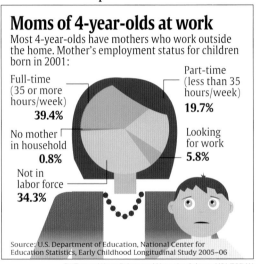

Moms of 4-year-olds at work

Most 4-year-olds have mothers who work outside the home. Mother's employment status for children born in 2001:

Full-time
(35 or more hours/week)
39.4%

Part-time
(less than 35 hours/week)
19.7%

No mother in household
0.8%

Looking for work
5.8%

Not in labor force
34.3%

Source: U.S. Department of Education, National Center for Education Statistics, Early Childhood Longitudinal Study 2005–06

By Tracey Wong Briggs and Veronica Salazar, USA TODAY

USA TODAY Snapshots®

Grocery shopping for the kids

Most important factors moms consider:

Taste **21%**

Child's preference **22%**

Price **17%**

Nutritional content **27%**

Source: Ronzoni Smart Taste survey of 1,000 mothers or female guardians of children ages 5 to 17 conducted by Synovate. Margin of error ±3 percentage points.

By Michelle Healy and Veronica Salazar, USA TODAY

USA TODAY Snapshots®

Calling for help

Where crisis callers to
the National Runaway
Switchboard called from:

Home **43%**

Friend's
place **21%**

Street/
Pay phone **9%**

Relative's
home **5%**

1-800-RUNAWAY
Source: National Runaway Switchboard

By David Stuckey and Veronica Salazar, USA TODAY

▥ Home

What did you spend on your first home purchase? Are you curious to learn what others have spent? Depending on where you live, owning may be more or less common: 81 percent of West Virginia's populace own, versus 55 percent of New York's. And depending on where you live, the cost of that home will vary significantly. Do you live in one of the five cities with the costliest homes? One of the five cities with the lowest priced homes? Where are homes losing value? Where can you buy the safest bet?

What sorts of things do you keep in your home? Where do you pay the bills? Do you clean some rooms more often than others? How prepared are you in case of an emergency? What convenience do you wish for most? What kinds of household inventions would you dream up? What would your neighbors say?

What do you think?

USA TODAY Snapshots®

What first-time home buyers pay

Prices of homes purchased by first-time buyers:

$100,001 to $200,000 **45%**

Less than
$100,000
19%

$200,001
to
$300,000
20%

$300,001
to
$400,000
8%

More than
$400,001 **10%**

SOLD

Note: Total doesn't add up to 100 due to rounding
Source: National Association of Realtors Profile of Home Buyers and Sellers

By Jae Yang and Bob Laird, USA TODAY

USA TODAY Snapshots®

Measuring your CO₂ footprint

Have you ever used an online calculator to figure your personal or your household's carbon footprint (the amount of heat-trapping carbon dioxide released into the atmosphere)?

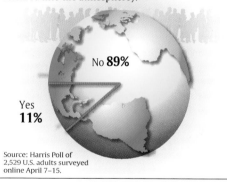

No **89%**

Yes
11%

Source: Harris Poll of
2,529 U.S. adults surveyed
online April 7–15.

By Michelle Healy and Julie Snider, USA TODAY

USA TODAY Snapshots®

Selling home for long-term care

Do you think you may have to sell your home to pay for long-term care in your retirement?

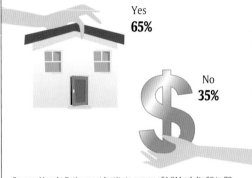

Yes
65%

No
35%

Source: Lincoln Retirement Institute survey of 1,011 adults 50 to 70 years old. Margin of error ±3 percentage points.

By Jae Yang and Veronica Salazar, USA TODAY

USA TODAY Snapshots®

Cities with costliest homes

City, cost of the median three-bedroom and two-bath home:

Tomorrow: Five least-expensive cities

$816,022

$670,959

$624,466

$527,908

$486,556

| Santa Barbara, Santa Maria, Lompoc, Calif. | San Francisco, Oakland, San Jose, Calif. | Honolulu | Los Angeles, Riverside, Orange County, Calif. | San Diego |

Source: Zillow.com

By Jae Yang and Karl Gelles, USA TODAY

USA TODAY Snapshots®

Cities with lower-cost homes

City, cost of the median three-bedroom and two-bath home:

$97,059 — Tulsa
$109,658 — Columbia, S.C.
$123,833 — Cleveland-Akron, Ohio
$126,961 — Columbus, Ohio
$132,565 — Pensacola, Fla.

Source: Zillow.com

By Jae Yang and Marcy E. Mullins, USA TODAY

180

USA TODAY Snapshots®

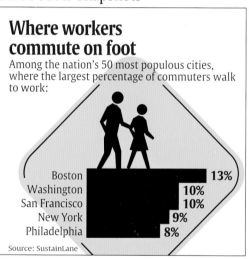

Where workers commute on foot

Among the nation's 50 most populous cities, where the largest percentage of commuters walk to work:

Boston 13%
Washington 10%
San Francisco 10%
New York 9%
Philadelphia 8%

Source: SustainLane

By Anne R. Carey and Adrienne Lewis, USA TODAY

USA TODAY Snapshots®

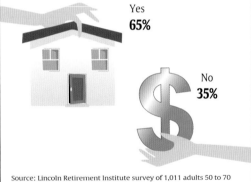

Selling home for long-term care

Do you think you may have to sell your home to pay for long-term care in your retirement?

Yes
65%

No
35%

Source: Lincoln Retirement Institute survey of 1,011 adults 50 to 70 years old. Margin of error ±3 percentage points.

By Jae Yang and Veronica Salazar, USA TODAY

USA TODAY Snapshots®

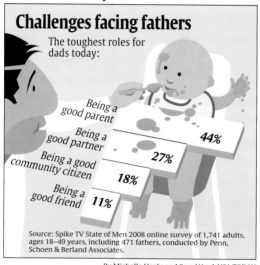

Challenges facing fathers

The toughest roles for dads today:

Being a good parent **44%**

Being a good partner **27%**

Being a good community citizen **18%**

Being a good friend **11%**

Source: Spike TV State of Men 2008 online survey of 1,741 adults, ages 18–49 years, including 471 fathers, conducted by Penn, Schoen & Berland Associates.

By Michelle Healy and Sam Ward, USA TODAY

USA TODAY Snapshots®

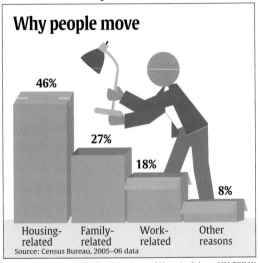

Why people move

46% Housing-related

27% Family-related

18% Work-related

8% Other reasons

Source: Census Bureau, 2005–06 data

By David Stuckey and Veronica Salazar, USA TODAY

184

USA TODAY Snapshots®

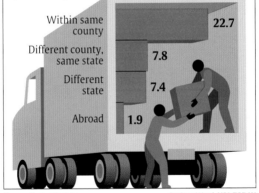

Mobile society

Nearly 40 million people, 14% of the U.S. population, moved between 2004 and 2005. Where they went: (in millions)

Within same county	22.7
Different county, same state	7.8
Different state	7.4
Abroad	1.9

Source: Census Bureau

By Sam Ward, USA TODAY

USA TODAY Snapshots®

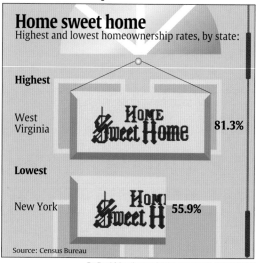

Home sweet home
Highest and lowest homeownership rates, by state:

Highest

West Virginia — 81.3%

Lowest

New York — 55.9%

Source: Census Bureau

By David Stuckey and Adrienne Lewis, USA TODAY

USA TODAY Snapshots®

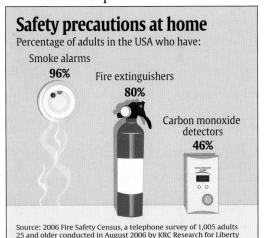

Safety precautions at home

Percentage of adults in the USA who have:

Smoke alarms
96%

Fire extinguishers
80%

Carbon monoxide detectors
46%

Source: 2006 Fire Safety Census, a telephone survey of 1,005 adults 25 and older conducted in August 2006 by KRC Research for Liberty Mutual and International Association of Fire Fighters. Margin of error ±3.1 percentage points.

By Tracey Wong Briggs and Veronica Salazar, USA TODAY

USA TODAY Snapshots®

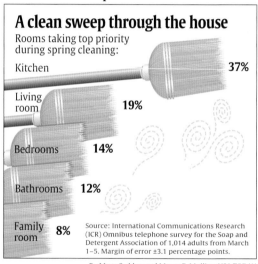

A clean sweep through the house

Rooms taking top priority
during spring cleaning:

Kitchen **37%**

Living room **19%**

Bedrooms **14%**

Bathrooms **12%**

Family room **8%**

Source: International Communications Research
(ICR) Omnibus telephone survey for the Soap and
Detergent Association of 1,014 adults from March
1–5. Margin of error ±3.1 percentage points.

By Mary Cadden and Marcy E. Mullins, USA TODAY

USA TODAY Snapshots®

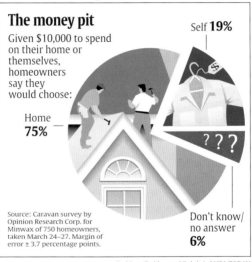

The money pit

Given $10,000 to spend on their home or themselves, homeowners say they would choose:

Self **19%**

Home
75%

???

Don't know/
no answer
6%

Source: Caravan survey by Opinion Research Corp. for Minwax of 750 homeowners, taken March 24–27. Margin of error ± 3.7 percentage points.

By Mary Cadden and Bob Laird USA TODAY

USA TODAY Snapshots®

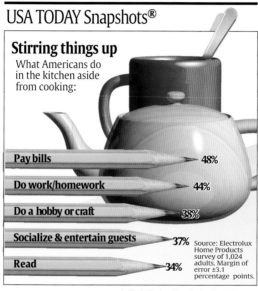

Stirring things up

What Americans do in the kitchen aside from cooking:

Pay bills	48%
Do work/homework	44%
Do a hobby or craft	38%
Socialize & entertain guests	37%
Read	34%

Source: Electrolux Home Products survey of 1,024 adults. Margin of error ±3.1 percentage points.

By Cindy Clark and Suzy Parker, USA TODAY

USA TODAY Snapshots®

Watch where you lay things
Top five possessions dog owners said their dogs damaged because of chewing habits:

Shoes 39%
Furniture 38%
Clothing 26%
Kids' toys 20%
Electronic equipment 15%

Source: TheHealthyChew.com   By David Stuckey and Dave Merrill, USA TODAY

USA TODAY Snapshots®

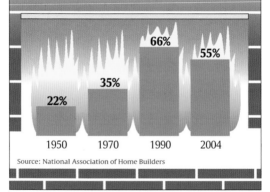

Warming up to fireplaces

Even though most homes in the USA have central air and heat, most new single-family homes have fireplaces. Percentage with at least one fireplace:

- 22% — 1950
- 35% — 1970
- 66% — 1990
- 55% — 2004

Source: National Association of Home Builders

By David Stuckey and Keith Simmons, USA TODAY

USA TODAY Snapshots®

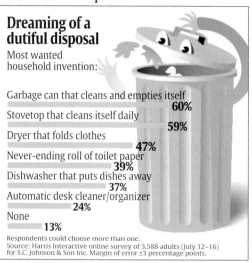

Dreaming of a dutiful disposal

Most wanted household invention:

Garbage can that cleans and empties itself
60%

Stovetop that cleans itself daily
59%

Dryer that folds clothes
47%

Never-ending roll of toilet paper
39%

Dishwasher that puts dishes away
37%

Automatic desk cleaner/organizer
24%

None
13%

Respondents could choose more than one.
Source: Harris Interactive online survey of 3,588 adults (July 12–16) for S.C. Johnson & Son Inc. Margin of error ±3 percentage points.

By Mary Cadden and Bob Laird, USA TODAY

USA TODAY Snapshots®

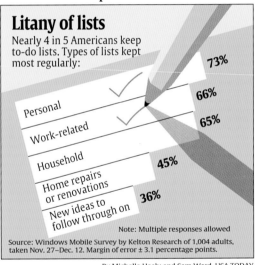

Litany of lists

Nearly 4 in 5 Americans keep to-do lists. Types of lists kept most regularly:

Personal — 73%

Work-related — 66%

Household — 65%

Home repairs or renovations — 45%

New ideas to follow through on — 36%

Note: Multiple responses allowed

Source: Windows Mobile Survey by Kelton Research of 1,004 adults, taken Nov. 27–Dec. 12. Margin of error ± 3.1 percentage points.

By Michelle Healy and Sam Ward, USA TODAY

USA TODAY Snapshots®

In case of emergency...

Slightly more than half (52%) of adults say they have disaster supply kits. Of those who have kits, items they say they definitely have:

Flashlight	**94%**
Extra batteries	**88%**
First aid kit	**85%**
Three-day supply of non-perishable food	**76%**
Three-day supply of water	**72%**
Battery or hand-crank radio	**71%**

Source: Telephone survey of 1,000 adults 18 years and older conducted by ORC International for the American Red Cross, May 4–7, 2006. Margin of error is ±3.1 percentage points overall, 6 percentage points for those who have kits.

By Tracey Wong Briggs and Marcy E. Mullins, USA TODAY

USA TODAY Snapshots®

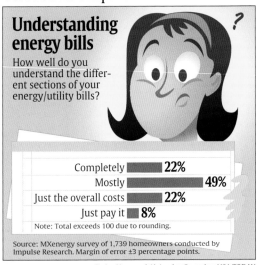

Understanding energy bills

How well do you understand the different sections of your energy/utility bills?

Completely	22%
Mostly	49%
Just the overall costs	22%
Just pay it	8%

Note: Total exceeds 100 due to rounding.

Source: MXenergy survey of 1,739 homeowners conducted by Impulse Research. Margin of error ±3 percentage points.

By Jae Yang and Alejandro Gonzalez, USA TODAY

USA TODAY Snapshots®

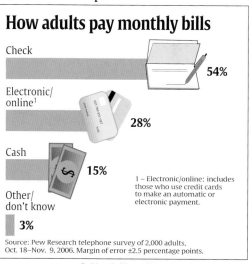

How adults pay monthly bills

Check
54%

Electronic/
online[1]
28%

Cash
15%

Other/
don't know
3%

1 – Electronic/online: includes
those who use credit cards
to make an automatic or
electronic payment.

Source: Pew Research telephone survey of 2,000 adults,
Oct. 18–Nov. 9, 2006. Margin of error ±2.5 percentage points.

By Mary Cadden and Veronica Salazar, USA TODAY

USA TODAY Snapshots®

The new New Orleans will rent like the big city

Projected 2007 fair-market rent for two-bedroom apartments in selected metropolitan areas:

Atlanta — $779
Las Vegas — $891
Philadelphia — $923
New Orleans — $978
New York — $1,189
Los Angeles — $1,269
Washington — $1,286

Source: Department of Housing and Urban Development

By David Stuckey and Marcy E. Mullins, USA TODAY

USA TODAY Snapshots®

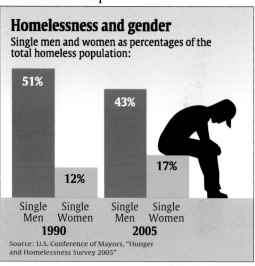

Homelessness and gender

Single men and women as percentages of the total homeless population:

51% — Single Men — 1990
12% — Single Women — 1990
43% — Single Men — 2005
17% — Single Women — 2005

Source: U.S. Conference of Mayors, "Hunger and Homelessness Survey 2005"

By Sam Ward, USA TODAY

USA TODAY Snapshots®

The pet story

Total number of pets owned in the USA (in millions):

Fish — 148.6

Cats — 90.5

Dogs — 73.9

Small animals — 18.2

Birds — 16.6

Reptiles — 11

Source: American Pet Product Manufacturers Association

By David Stuckey and Marcy E. Mullins, USA TODAY

USA TODAY Snapshots®

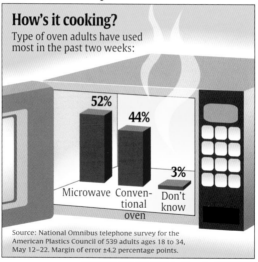

How's it cooking?

Type of oven adults have used most in the past two weeks:

52% Microwave
44% Conven-tional oven
3% Don't know

Source: National Omnibus telephone survey for the American Plastics Council of 539 adults ages 18 to 34, May 12–22. Margin of error ±4.2 percentage points.

By Mary Cadden and Alejandro Gonzalez, USA TODAY

USA TODAY Snapshots®

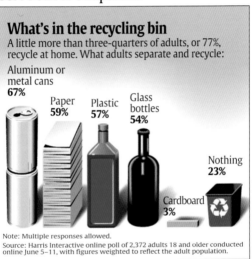

What's in the recycling bin

A little more than three-quarters of adults, or 77%, recycle at home. What adults separate and recycle:

Aluminum or metal cans
67%

Paper
59%

Plastic
57%

Glass bottles
54%

Nothing
23%

Cardboard
3%

Note: Multiple responses allowed.

Source: Harris Interactive online poll of 2,372 adults 18 and older conducted online June 5–11, with figures weighted to reflect the adult population.

By Tracey Wong Briggs and Bob Laird, USA TODAY

USA TODAY Snapshots®

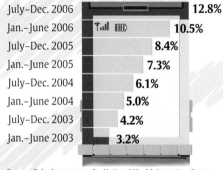

Going without a landline

The percentage of cellphone-only households has quadrupled in four years:

July–Dec. 2006	**12.8%**
Jan.–June 2006	**10.5%**
July–Dec. 2005	**8.4%**
Jan.–June 2005	**7.3%**
July–Dec. 2004	**6.1%**
Jan.–June 2004	**5.0%**
July–Dec. 2003	**4.2%**
Jan.–June 2003	**3.2%**

Source: Telephone status for National Health Interview Survey representing 13,056 households; Centers for Disease Control and Prevention

By Tracey Wong Briggs and Robert W. Ahrens, USA TODAY

USA TODAY Snapshots®

Fire starter
Percentage of home fires
originating in these rooms:

Kitchen — 34%

Bedroom — 12%

Living room, family room or den — 6%

Source: National Fire Protection Association

By David Stuckey and Robert W. Ahrens, USA TODAY

USA TODAY Snapshots®

Clicking on home improvement

Online retail spending on home
improvement products: (in billions)

2001 $1.8

2006 $13.6

Source: Jupiter Research

By David Stuckey and Robert W. Ahrens, USA TODAY

USA TODAY Snapshots®

Mowing don'ts
Adults who mow their yards said they:

Rarely use hearing protection — 79%

Listen to music — 28%

Drink beer — 12%

Source: *Consumer Reports.* National Research Center

By David Stuckey and Adrienne Lewis, USA TODAY

USA TODAY Snapshots®

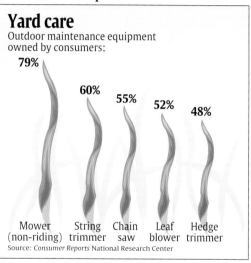

Yard care
Outdoor maintenance equipment
owned by consumers:

79%
60%
55%
52%
48%

Mower
(non-riding)
String
trimmer
Chain
saw
Leaf
blower
Hedge
trimmer

Source: *Consumer Reports* National Research Center

By David Stuckey and Robert W. Ahrens, USA TODAY

USA TODAY Snapshots®

Fire up the grill

More than two-thirds (68%) of Americans live in households that grill outdoors. Bad weather or extreme conditions under which they have grilled:

rain

68%

temperatures above 100°F

47%

temperatures below freezing

32%

snow, sleet or hail

26%

Source: Consumer Reports National Research Center telephone survey of 1,001 adults. Margin of error is ±3.2% percentage points

By Michelle Healy and Keith Simmons, USA TODAY

USA TODAY Snapshots®

Should the government help?

Should the government provide financial help to borrowers who can no longer afford to pay their mortgages to keep them out of foreclosure?

42%

33%

25%

Yes   No   Not sure

Source: Harris Interactive survey of 2,082 adults 18 and older; survey weighted to represent actual population

By Jae Yang and Robert W. Ahrens, USA TODAY

209

USA TODAY Snapshots®

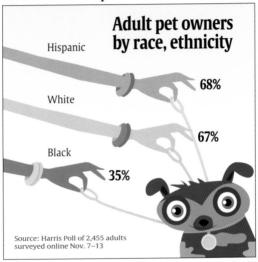

Adult pet owners by race, ethnicity

Hispanic 68%

White 67%

Black 35%

Source: Harris Poll of 2,455 adults surveyed online Nov. 7–13

By Michelle Healy and Veronica Salazar, USA TODAY

USA TODAY Snapshots®

A place to store stuff

What Americans value most in their dream homes:

Built-in storage — **63%**

Bathroom connected to every bedroom — **24%**

High-tech features[1] — **12%**

Luxury appointments[2] — **2%**

1 – includes security video monitors, surround sound, Internet connections.
2 – includes gold-plated faucets, crystal chandeliers, marble floors.

Note: Total does not add up to 100 due to rounding.
Source: Beazer Homes survey of 548 adults with a minimum annual household income of $40,000, conducted by MarketTools.
Margin of error ± 3 percentage points.

By Michelle Healy and Sam Ward USA TODAY

▨ Leisure

Attendance to theme parks, like Disneyland and Six Flags, is higher than ever! What else is everyone doing with their free time? What are you doing? Do you go camping? Do you like to fish? Have you gone skiing or snowboarding recently? Do you own a recreation vehicle? How often do you dine out? How often do you go to the movies?

How many hours do you think the typical American spends in front of the television each year? Can you estimate how many hours you spend? How do you get your daily news? Do you surf the Web even when you don't have a specific destination? Are men or women more likely to read literature?

How does your downtime measure up?

USA TODAY Snapshots®

Savoring the great outdoors

If you were participating in an outdoor recreational activity, what would you look forward to the most?

Exercise **38%**

Inspiration **11%**

Solitude **12%**

Forgetting about work **18%**

Companionship **21%**

Source: Open Air Magazine survey of 1,027 adults conducted by International Communications Research and co-sponsored by CGPR. Margin of error is ± 3 percentage points.

By Michelle Healy and Alejandro Gonzalez, USA TODAY

USA TODAY Snapshots®

Tranquility gardens

Nearly 8 in 10 adults say they have spent time with plants or gardened (indoors or outdoors) in the past year. Top reasons:

89%
Exposes me to fresh air and sunlight

83%
Provides a chance to spend time outside

79%
Provides a sense of accomplish-ment

78%
Makes me feel relaxed

Source: Scotts Miracle-Gro online survey of 1,000 adults. Margin of error ±3.1 percentage points.

By Michelle Healy and Karl Gelles, USA TODAY

USA TODAY Snapshots®

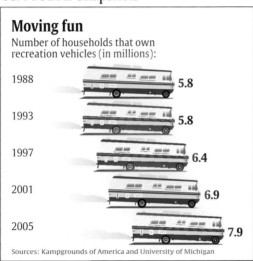

Moving fun

Number of households that own
recreation vehicles (in millions):

1988   **5.8**

1993   **5.8**

1997   **6.4**

2001   **6.9**

2005   **7.9**

Sources: Kampgrounds of America and University of Michigan

By David Stuckey and Karl Gelles, USA TODAY

USA TODAY Snapshots®

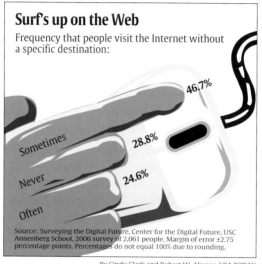

Surf's up on the Web

Frequency that people visit the Internet without a specific destination:

46.7%

Sometimes 28.8%

Never 24.6%

Often

Source: Surveying the Digital Future, Center for the Digital Future, USC Annenberg School, 2006 survey of 2,061 people. Margin of error ±2.75 percentage points. Percentages do not equal 100% due to rounding.

By Cindy Clark and Robert W. Ahrens, USA TODAY

USA TODAY Snapshots®

The screaming never stops
USA amusement/theme park attendance:
(in millions)

280 290 300 300 317 319 324 322 328 335

1995 1996 1997 1998 2000 2001 2002 2003 2004 2005

Source: International Association of Amusement Parks and Attractions

By David Stuckey and Bob Laird, USA TODAY

USA TODAY Snapshots®

Young Americans staying home
Percentage of Americans ages 18 to 24 who have traveled outside the USA in the past three years (by number of trips):

None **70%**

Three or more **9%**

Two **7%**

One **14%**

Source: National Geographic, *2006 Geographic Literacy Study*

By David Stuckey and Suzy Parker, USA TODAY

USA TODAY Snapshots®

Seized before flights

Number of prohibited items intercepted at
U.S. airport screening checkpoints:

2002	4,185,916
2003	6,167,497
2004	7,103,560

Source: Transportation Security Administration

By David Stuckey and Karl Gelles, USA TODAY

USA TODAY Snapshots®

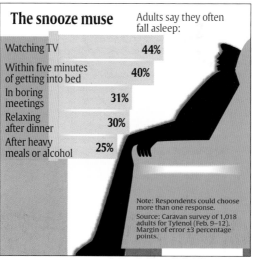

The snooze muse

Adults say they often fall asleep:

Watching TV — **44%**

Within five minutes of getting into bed — **40%**

In boring meetings — **31%**

Relaxing after dinner — **30%**

After heavy meals or alcohol — **25%**

Note: Respondents could choose more than one response.

Source: Caravan survey of 1,018 adults for Tylenol (Feb. 9–12). Margin of error ±3 percentage points.

By Mary Cadden and Julie Snider, USA TODAY

USA TODAY Snapshots®

Running through our dreams
Actions adults say they do in their dreams:

Chasing/being chased **37%**
Falling **28%**
Wading or swimming **15%**
Being invisible **9%**

Note: Respondents could choose more than one response.

Source: Harris Interactive QuickQuery of 3,152 adults for Select Comfort (March 23–27). Margin of error ±3 percentage points.

By Mary Cadden and Marcy E. Mullins, USA TODAY

USA TODAY Snapshots®

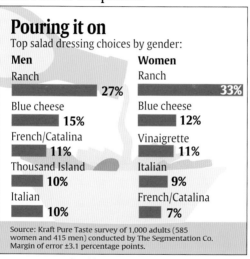

Pouring it on
Top salad dressing choices by gender:

Men

Ranch
27%

Blue cheese
15%

French/Catalina
11%

Thousand Island
10%

Italian
10%

Women

Ranch
33%

Blue cheese
12%

Vinaigrette
11%

Italian
9%

French/Catalina
7%

Source: Kraft Pure Taste survey of 1,000 adults (585 women and 415 men) conducted by The Segmentation Co. Margin of error ±3.1 percentage points.

By Michelle Healy and Adrienne Lewis, USA TODAY

USA TODAY Snapshots®

Reading fine prints

Percentage of people surveyed in 2002 who read literature at least once in the previous 12 months:

55%

Women

38%

Men

Source: Census Bureau   By David Stuckey and Marcy E. Mullins, USA TODAY

USA TODAY Snapshots®

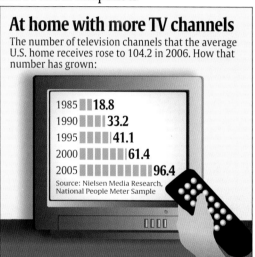

At home with more TV channels

The number of television channels that the average U.S. home receives rose to 104.2 in 2006. How that number has grown:

1985 | 18.8
1990 | 33.2
1995 | 41.1
2000 | 61.4
2005 | 96.4

Source: Nielsen Media Research, National People Meter Sample

By Cindy Clark and Alejandro Gonzalez, USA TODAY

USA TODAY Snapshots®

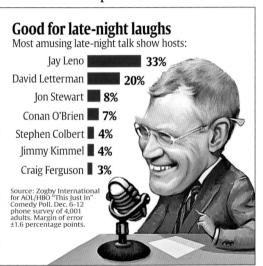

Good for late-night laughs
Most amusing late-night talk show hosts:

Jay Leno	33%
David Letterman	20%
Jon Stewart	8%
Conan O'Brien	7%
Stephen Colbert	4%
Jimmy Kimmel	4%
Craig Ferguson	3%

Source: Zogby International for AOL/HBO "This Just In" Comedy Poll. Dec. 6-12 phone survey of 4,001 adults. Margin of error ±1.6 percentage points.

By Cindy Clark and Keith Simmons, USA TODAY

USA TODAY Snapshots®

Who's tuned in to the MTV Movie Awards?

Number of viewers who watched winners take home the Golden Popcorn (in millions) at the MTV Movie Awards, which features such categories as Best Kiss.

7.1

5.9   5.9

4.7

3.2

'02   '03   '04   '05   '06

Source: Nielsen Media Research

By Cindy Clark and Sam Ward, USA TODAY

USA TODAY Snapshots®

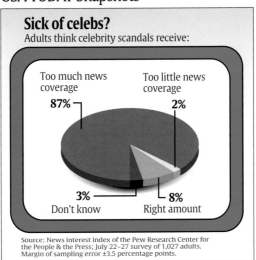

Sick of celebs?
Adults think celebrity scandals receive:

Too much news
coverage
87%

Too little news
coverage
2%

3%
Don't know

8%
Right amount

Source: News Interest Index of the Pew Research Center for
the People & the Press; July 22–27 survey of 1,027 adults.
Margin of sampling error ±3.5 percentage points.

By Cindy Clark and Keith Simmons, USA TODAY

USA TODAY Snapshots®

Republicans less likely to be fans of network news

Percentage of Americans who have a "favorable" opinion of network TV news coverage, by political party affiliation:

Democrats
84%

Independents
70%

Republicans
56%

Source: The Pew Research Center for the People & the Press survey of 1,503 adults July 25–29. Margin of error ±3 percentage points.

By Alejandro Gonzalez, USA TODAY

USA TODAY Snapshots®

Drinking by young adults

More than half of all adults 18–22 surveyed in 2005 said they had engaged in binge drinking or heavy drinking in the past month. How full-time college students compared with others in their age group:

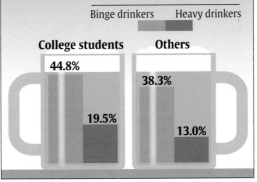

Binge drinkers   Heavy drinkers

College students   **Others**

44.8%

38.3%

19.5%

13.0%

Source: National Survey on Drug Use and Health   By Sam Ward, USA TODAY

USA TODAY Snapshots®

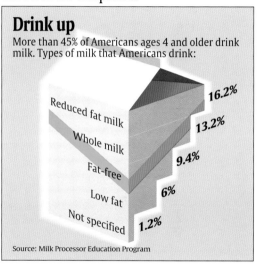

Drink up

More than 45% of Americans ages 4 and older drink milk. Types of milk that Americans drink:

Reduced fat milk — 16.2%

Whole milk — 13.2%

Fat-free — 9.4%

Low fat — 6%

Not specified — 1.2%

Source: Milk Processor Education Program

By David Stuckey and Adrienne Lewis, USA TODAY

USA TODAY Snapshots®

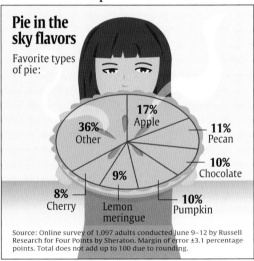

Pie in the sky flavors

Favorite types of pie:

- 17% Apple
- 36% Other
- 11% Pecan
- 10% Chocolate
- 8% Cherry
- 9% Lemon meringue
- 10% Pumpkin

Source: Online survey of 1,097 adults conducted June 9–12 by Russell Research for Four Points by Sheraton. Margin of error ±3.1 percentage points. Total does not add up to 100 due to rounding.

By Mary Cadden and Veronica Salazar, USA TODAY

USA TODAY Snapshots®

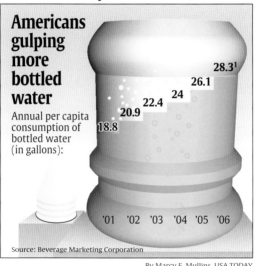

Americans gulping more bottled water

Annual per capita consumption of bottled water (in gallons):

18.8   20.9   22.4   24   26.1   28.3[1]

'01   '02   '03   '04   '05   '06

Source: Beverage Marketing Corporation

By Marcy E. Mullins, USA TODAY

USA TODAY Snapshots®

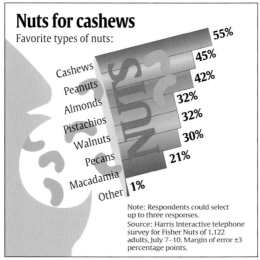

Nuts for cashews

Favorite types of nuts:

Cashews 55%
Peanuts 45%
Almonds 42%
Pistachios 32%
Walnuts 32%
Pecans 30%
Macadamia 21%
Other 1%

Note: Respondents could select up to three responses.

Source: Harris Interactive telephone survey for Fisher Nuts of 1,122 adults, July 7–10. Margin of error ±3 percentage points.

By Mary Cadden and Adrienne Lewis, USA TODAY

USA TODAY Snapshots®

Hot on the grill

Most popular foods for barbecuing:

87% Hamburgers

83% Steak

78% Chicken

76% Hot dogs

Source: Hearth, Patio & Barbecue Association

By David Stuckey and Karl Gelles, USA TODAY

235

USA TODAY Snapshots®

Our daily sandwich bread

Seventy-two percent of adults eat sandwiches at least once a week. Types of bread most likely to be used:

Wheat bread	**67%**
White bread	**43%**
Bun or roll	**27%**
Rye	**18%**
Pita/wrap	**15%**
Pumpernickel	**6%**

Source: Harris Interactive Quick Query online survey of 2,604 people for Grain Foods from July 27–31. Margin of error ±3 percentage points. Respondents could choose more than one.

By Mary Cadden and Veronica Salazar, USA TODAY

USA TODAY Snapshots®

Biting into chocolate

Annual pounds per capita consumed in selected countries:

Switzerland **22.7**

United Kingdom **18.5**

Belgium **15**

USA **12.1**

Japan **4**

Source: Business Monitor International

By Marcy E. Mullins, USA TODAY

USA TODAY Snapshots®

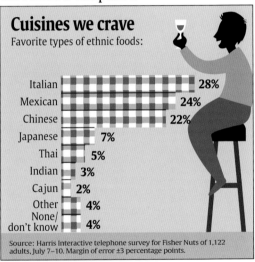

Cuisines we crave

Favorite types of ethnic foods:

Cuisine	Percentage
Italian	28%
Mexican	24%
Chinese	22%
Japanese	7%
Thai	5%
Indian	3%
Cajun	2%
Other	4%
None/don't know	4%

Source: Harris Interactive telephone survey for Fisher Nuts of 1,122 adults, July 7–10. Margin of error ±3 percentage points.

By Mary Cadden and Sam Ward, USA TODAY

USA TODAY Snapshots®

Summer! Hot Dog!

Americans typically consume 7 billion hot dogs from Memorial Day through Labor Day. (Average annual consumption: 20 billion)

That's **818** hot dogs every second during the summer.

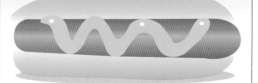

Sources: National Hot Dog & Sausage Council; American Meat Institute

By Anne R. Carey and Keith Simmons, USA TODAY

USA TODAY Snapshots®

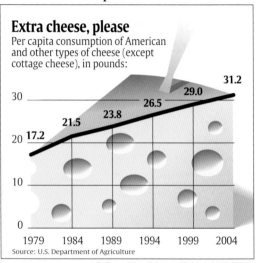

Extra cheese, please

Per capita consumption of American and other types of cheese (except cottage cheese), in pounds:

- 17.2 (1979)
- 21.5 (1984)
- 23.8 (1989)
- 26.5 (1994)
- 29.0 (1999)
- 31.2 (2004)

Source: U.S. Department of Agriculture

By Tracey Wong Briggs and Bob Laird, USA TODAY

240

USA TODAY Snapshots®

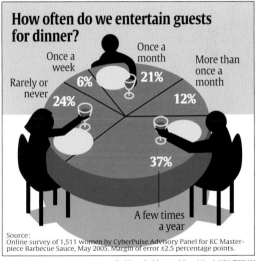

How often do we entertain guests for dinner?

Once a week **6%**

Once a month **21%**

More than once a month **12%**

Rarely or never **24%**

A few times a year **37%**

Source:
Online survey of 1,511 women by CyberPulse Advisory Panel for KC Master-piece Barbecue Sauce, May 2005. Margin of error ±2.5 percentage points.

By Mary Cadden and Sam Ward, USA TODAY

USA TODAY Snapshots®

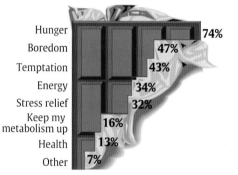

Triggering a snack attack
Why adults snack:

Hunger — 74%
Boredom — 47%
Temptation — 43%
Energy — 34%
Stress relief — 32%
Keep my metabolism up — 16%
Health — 13%
Other — 7%

Note: Respondents could choose more than one.
Source: Harris Interactive survey of 2,915 adults, May 10–14 for Mullen Public Relations. Margin of error ±3 percentage points.

By Mary Cadden and Robert W. Ahrens, USA TODAY

USA TODAY Snapshots®

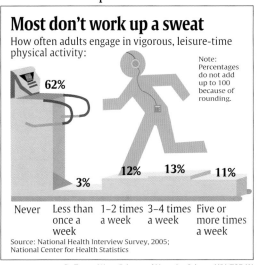

Most don't work up a sweat

How often adults engage in vigorous, leisure-time physical activity:

Note: Percentages do not add up to 100 because of rounding.

62%

3%

12%

13%

11%

| Never | Less than once a week | 1–2 times a week | 3–4 times a week | Five or more times a week |

Source: National Health Interview Survey, 2005; National Center for Health Statistics

By Tracey Wong Briggs and Veronica Salazar, USA TODAY

USA TODAY Snapshots®

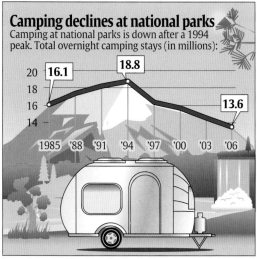

Camping declines at national parks
Camping at national parks is down after a 1994 peak. Total overnight camping stays (in millions):

16.1   18.8   13.6

1985 '88 '91 '94 '97 '00 '03 '06

Source: National Park Service   By Mary Cadden and Dave Merrill, USA TODAY

USA TODAY Snapshots®

Skyrocketing July 4th fireworks

Which city's fireworks display would you most like to see this Independence Day?

New York
25%

Washington, D.C.
17%

Chicago
7%

Boston, Los Angeles, Philadelphia (tie)
6%

Other
32%

Note: Total doesn't add up to 100 because of rounding.

Source: Travelzoo.com survey of 1,000 adults conducted by Wakefield

By Michelle Healy and Alejandro Gonzalez, USA TODAY

USA TODAY Snapshots®

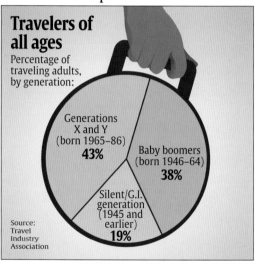

Travelers of all ages

Percentage of traveling adults, by generation:

Generations X and Y (born 1965–86) **43%**

Baby boomers (born 1946–64) **38%**

Silent/G.I. generation (1945 and earlier) **19%**

Source: Travel Industry Association

By David Stuckey and Alejandro Gonzalez, USA TODAY

USA TODAY Snapshots®

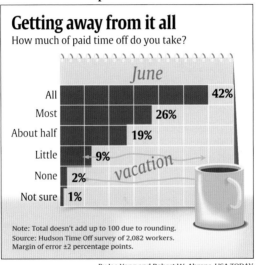

Getting away from it all

How much of paid time off do you take?

All	42%
Most	26%
About half	19%
Little	9%
None	2%
Not sure	1%

Note: Total doesn't add up to 100 due to rounding.
Source: Hudson Time Off survey of 2,082 workers.
Margin of error ±2 percentage points.

By Jae Yang and Robert W. Ahrens, USA TODAY

USA TODAY Snapshots®

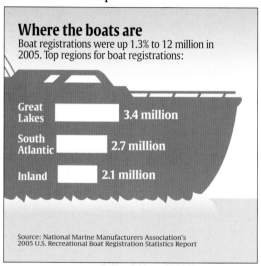

Where the boats are
Boat registrations were up 1.3% to 12 million in 2005. Top regions for boat registrations:

Great Lakes	3.4 million
South Atlantic	2.7 million
Inland	2.1 million

Source: National Marine Manufacturers Association's
2005 U.S. Recreational Boat Registration Statistics Report

By Mary Cadden and Keith Simmons, USA TODAY

USA TODAY Snapshots®

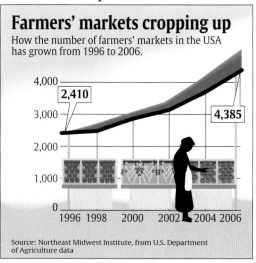

Farmers' markets cropping up

How the number of farmers' markets in the USA has grown from 1996 to 2006.

2,410

4,385

4,000
3,000
2,000
1,000
0

1996 1998 2000 2002 2004 2006

Source: Northeast Midwest Institute, from U.S. Department of Agriculture data

By Mary Cadden and Robert W. Ahrens, USA TODAY

USA TODAY Snapshots®

Please pass the fresh veggies

Per capita consumption of fresh vegetables, in pounds per year[1]:

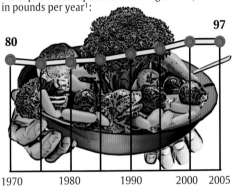

80

97

1970   1980   1990   2000   2005

1– Per capita availability adjusted for loss from farm to table.
Source: U.S. Department of Agriculture/Economuc Research Service

By Tracey Wong Briggs and Suzy Parker, USA TODAY

USA TODAY Snapshots®

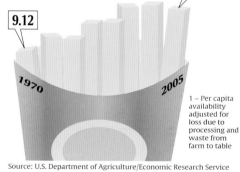

Want fries with that? Heck, yeah!

Fueled by the popularity of fast-food fries, consumption of frozen potatoes has boomed. Per capita consumption in pounds per year[1]:

17.48

9.12

1970

2005

1 – Per capita availability adjusted for loss due to processing and waste from farm to table

Source: U.S. Department of Agriculture/Economic Research Service

By Tracey Wong Briggs and Veronica Salazar, USA TODAY

USA TODAY Snapshots®

State of quarter collecting

Number of adults who collect state quarters (in millions):

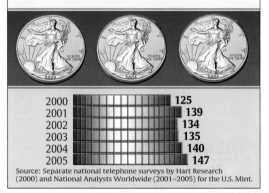

Year	Millions
2000	125
2001	139
2002	134
2003	135
2004	140
2005	147

Source: Separate national telephone surveys by Hart Research (2000) and National Analysts Worldwide (2001–2005) for the U.S. Mint.

By Tracey Wong Briggs and Suzy Parker, USA TODAY

USA TODAY Snapshots®

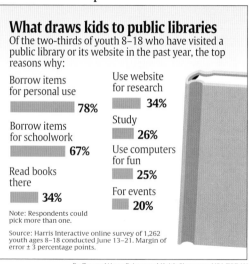

What draws kids to public libraries

Of the two-thirds of youth 8–18 who have visited a public library or its website in the past year, the top reasons why:

Borrow items
for personal use
78%

Borrow items
for schoolwork
67%

Read books
there
34%

Use website
for research
34%

Study
26%

Use computers
for fun
25%

For events
20%

Note: Respondents could pick more than one.

Source: Harris Interactive online survey of 1,262 youth ages 8–18 conducted June 13–21. Margin of error ± 3 percentage points.

By Tracey Wong Briggs and Keith Simmons, USA TODAY

USA TODAY Snapshots®

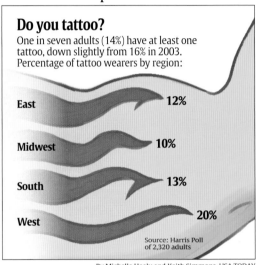

Do you tattoo?

One in seven adults (14%) have at least one tattoo, down slightly from 16% in 2003. Percentage of tattoo wearers by region:

East 12%

Midwest 10%

South 13%

West 20%

Source: Harris Poll of 2,320 adults

By Michelle Healy and Keith Simmons, USA TODAY

USA TODAY Snapshots®

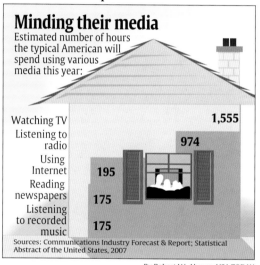

Minding their media
Estimated number of hours the typical American will spend using various media this year:

Watching TV	1,555
Listening to radio	974
Using Internet	195
Reading newspapers	175
Listening to recorded music	175

Sources: Communications Industry Forecast & Report; Statistical Abstract of the United States, 2007

By Robert W. Ahrens, USA TODAY

USA TODAY Snapshots®

In the down time

Percentage of adults who participated in top leisure activities at least once in previous 12 months:

Activity	Percentage
Dining out	48%
Entertaining friends or relatives at home	38%
Reading books	35%
Barbecuing	34%
Surfing the Net	28%

Source: Census Bureau

By David Stuckey and Marcy E. Mullins, USA TODAY

USA TODAY Snapshots®

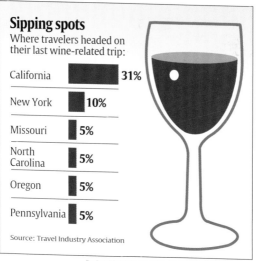

Sipping spots
Where travelers headed on
their last wine-related trip:

California	**31%**
New York	**10%**
Missouri	**5%**
North Carolina	**5%**
Oregon	**5%**
Pennsylvania	**5%**

Source: Travel Industry Association

By David Stuckey and Keith Simmons, USA TODAY

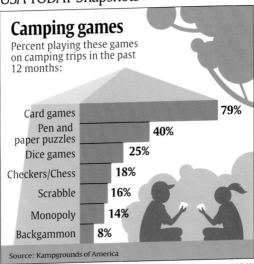

USA TODAY Snapshots®

Camping games

Percent playing these games on camping trips in the past 12 months:

Game	Percent
Card games	79%
Pen and paper puzzles	40%
Dice games	25%
Checkers/Chess	18%
Scrabble	16%
Monopoly	14%
Backgammon	8%

Source: Kampgrounds of America

By David Stuckey and Sam Ward, USA TODAY

USA TODAY Snapshots®

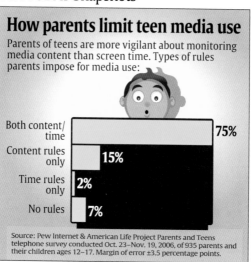

How parents limit teen media use

Parents of teens are more vigilant about monitoring media content than screen time. Types of rules parents impose for media use:

Both content/time	75%
Content rules only	15%
Time rules only	2%
No rules	7%

Source: Pew Internet & American Life Project Parents and Teens telephone survey conducted Oct. 23–Nov. 19, 2006, of 935 parents and their children ages 12–17. Margin of error ±3.5 percentage points.

By Cindy Clark and Alejandro Gonzalez, USA TODAY

USA TODAY Snapshots®

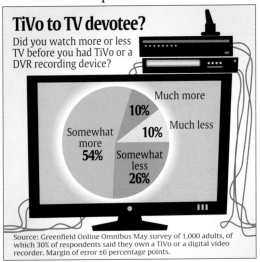

TiVo to TV devotee?

Did you watch more or less TV before you had TiVo or a DVR recording device?

Much more
10%

Much less
10%

Somewhat more
54%

Somewhat less
26%

Source: Greenfield Online Omnibus May survey of 1,000 adults, of which 30% of respondents said they own a TiVo or a digital video recorder. Margin of error ±6 percentage points.

By Cindy Clark and Alejandro Gonzalez, USA TODAY

USA TODAY Snapshots®

Running through our dreams
Actions adults say they do in their dreams:

Chasing/being chased — 37%
Falling — 28%
Wading or swimming — 15%
Being invisible — 9%

Note: Respondents could choose more than one response

Source: Harris Interactive QuickQuery of 3,152 adults for Select Comfort (March 23–27). Margin or error ±3 percentage points.

By Mary Cadden and Marcy E. Mullins, USA TODAY

USA TODAY Snapshots®

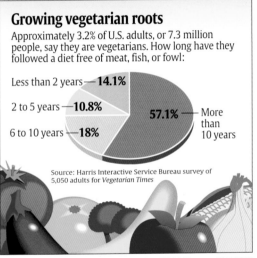

Growing vegetarian roots

Approximately 3.2% of U.S. adults, or 7.3 million people, say they are vegetarians. How long have they followed a diet free of meat, fish, or fowl:

Less than 2 years — **14.1%**

2 to 5 years — **10.8%**

6 to 10 years — **18%**

57.1% — More than 10 years

Source: Harris Interactive Service Bureau survey of 5,050 adults for *Vegetarian Times*

By Michelle Healy and Keith Simmons, USA TODAY

USA TODAY Snapshots®

Getting crafty

Nearly $32 billion is spent annually by crafting enthusiasts in the USA. The most popular crafts, by dollar sales (in billions):

Scrapbooking	$2.6
Art and drawing	$2.0
Painting and finishing	$1.9
Home décor	$1.5
Woodworking	$1.3

Source: Craft & Hobby Association Attitude & Usage Study, 2007

By Michelle Healy and Suzy Parker, USA TODAY

■ Technology

Have you ever downloaded something without paying, even when you know you should have paid? How many times a week do you log on to free content-sharing sites like YouTube? Do you shop online? More or less than everyone else? Do you frequently visit a social networking site? How many "friends" do you have on your Facebook or MySpace page? On your AIM buddy list? In your e-mail contact book? How many does the average teenager have in his or hers?

Though not all of us maintain a personal networking page, most of us seem to be tied to our cellphones 24/7. What device would you feel naked leaving the house without? How many text messages do you send in a day? Do you volunteer—or are you required—to stay connected to work even when you're away from your desk? Are you more likely to read the news on a screen or in print? What product's recent debut was most notable, in your opinion?

Are you tuned in to tech trends?

USA TODAY Snapshots®

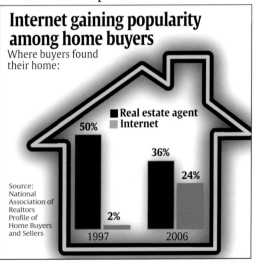

Internet gaining popularity among home buyers

Where buyers found their home:

■ Real estate agent
■ Internet

Source: National Association of Realtors Profile of Home Buyers and Sellers

1997: 50%, 2%
2006: 36%, 24%

By Jae Yang and Suzy Parker, USA TODAY

USA TODAY Snapshots®

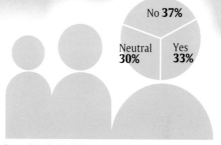

What the boss might see

If you knew your employer could see content from your social network website such as MySpace, Friendster or Facebook, would you remove any content from it?

No **37%**

Neutral **30%**

Yes **33%**

Source: Spherion Workplace survey of 1,601 employed adults 18 and older. Margin of error ±3 percentage points.

By Jae Yang and Robert W. Ahrens, USA TODAY

USA TODAY Snapshots®

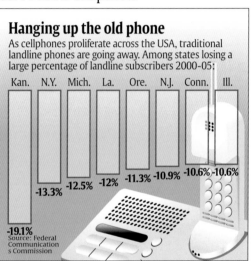

Hanging up the old phone

As cellphones proliferate across the USA, traditional landline phones are going away. Among states losing a large percentage of landline subscribers 2000-05:

Kan. N.Y. Mich. La. Ore. N.J. Conn. Ill.

-13.3% -12.5% -12% -11.3% -10.9% -10.6% -10.6%

-19.1%
Source: Federal Communications Commission

By Marcy E. Mullins, USA TODAY

USA TODAY Snapshots®

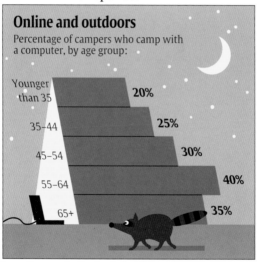

Online and outdoors

Percentage of campers who camp with a computer, by age group:

Younger than 35 — **20%**

35–44 — **25%**

45–54 — **30%**

55–64 — **40%**

65+ — **35%**

Source: Kampgrounds of America   By David Stuckey and Sam Ward, USA TODAY

269

USA TODAY Snapshots®

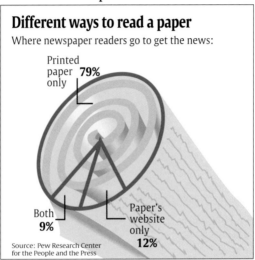

Different ways to read a paper

Where newspaper readers go to get the news:

Printed paper only **79%**

Both **9%**

Paper's website only **12%**

Source: Pew Research Center for the People and the Press

By David Stuckey and Adrienne Lewis, USA TODAY

USA TODAY Snapshots®

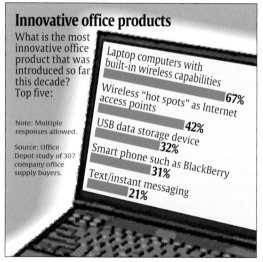

Innovative office products

What is the most innovative office product that was introduced so far this decade? Top five:

Note: Multiple responses allowed.

Source: Office Depot study of 307 company office supply buyers.

Laptop computers with built-in wireless capabilities **67%**

Wireless "hot spots" as Internet access points **42%**

USB data storage device **32%**

Smart phone such as BlackBerry **31%**

Text/instant messaging **21%**

By Jae Yang and Alejandro Gonzalez, USA TODAY

271

USA TODAY Snapshots®

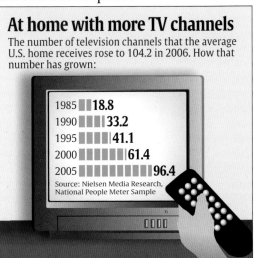

At home with more TV channels

The number of television channels that the average U.S. home receives rose to 104.2 in 2006. How that number has grown:

1985　18.8
1990　33.2
1995　41.1
2000　61.4
2005　96.4

Source: Nielsen Media Research, National People Meter Sample

By Cindy Clark and Alejandro Gonzalez, USA TODAY

USA TODAY Snapshots®

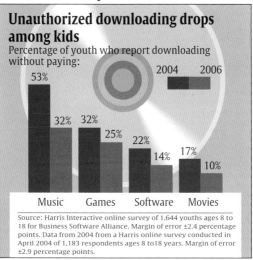

Unauthorized downloading drops among kids

Percentage of youth who report downloading without paying:

2004 2006

	Music	Games	Software	Movies
2004	53%	32%	22%	17%
2006	32%	25%	14%	10%

Source: Harris Interactive online survey of 1,644 youths ages 8 to 18 for Business Software Alliance. Margin of error ±2.4 percentage points. Data from 2004 from a Harris online survey conducted in April 2004 of 1,183 respondents ages 8 to18 years. Margin of error ±2.9 percentage points.

By Cindy Clark and Sam Ward, USA TODAY

USA TODAY Snapshots®

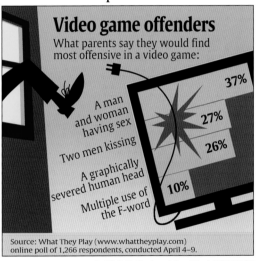

Video game offenders

What parents say they would find most offensive in a video game:

A man and woman having sex — 37%

Two men kissing — 27%

A graphically severed human head — 26%

Multiple use of the F-word — 10%

Source: What They Play (www.whattheyplay.com) online poll of 1,266 respondents, conducted April 4–9.

By Michelle Healy and Sam Ward, USA TODAY

USA TODAY Snapshots®

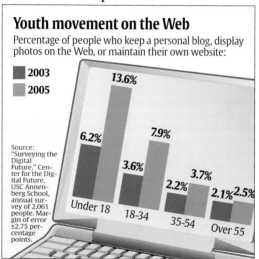

Youth movement on the Web

Percentage of people who keep a personal blog, display photos on the Web, or maintain their own website:

- 2003
- 2005

13.6%

6.2%

7.9%

3.6%

2.2%

3.7%

2.1% 2.5%

Under 18   18-34   35-54   Over 55

Source: "Surveying the Digital Future," Center for the Digital Future, USC Annenberg School, annual survey of 2,061 people. Margin of error ±2.75 percentage points.

By Cindy Clark and Marcy E. Mullins, USA TODAY

USA TODAY Snapshots®

**Majority feel technology[1]
has not improved customer
service in past five years.**

Don't know
2%

Dissatisfied
61%

Satisfied
37%

1—Includes automated phone service,
live chat via the Internet, etc.

Source: Accenture survey of 2,025 respondents 18
or older. Margin of error ±2 percentage points.

By Jae Yang and Suzy Parker, USA TODAY

USA TODAY Snapshots®

How wired are teens and their parents?

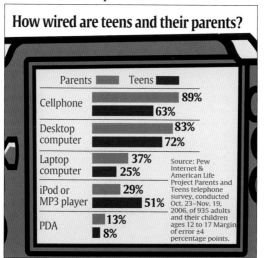

Parents ▮ Teens ▮

Cellphone	Parents 89% / Teens 63%
Desktop computer	Parents 83% / Teens 72%
Laptop computer	Parents 37% / Teens 25%
iPod or MP3 player	Parents 29% / Teens 51%
PDA	Parents 13% / Teens 8%

Source: Pew Internet & American Life Project Parents and Teens telephone survey, conducted Oct. 23–Nov. 19, 2006, of 935 adults and their children ages 12 to 17 Margin of error ±4 percentage points.

By Cindy Clark and Keith Simmons, USA TODAY

USA TODAY Snapshots®

Kids' technology use influences parents

Gen Xers (born 1965 to 1981) with millennial kids (9–28) at home are more likely to have portable digital media players such as iPods.

Portable digital media player ownership:

Gen Xers with
millennial kids at home **19%**

Gen Xers without
millennial kids at home **10%**

Source: Millennial Strategy Program
research online survey of 537 Gen
Xers and 2,101 millennials. Gen Xers
margin of error is ±4.5 percentage
points; millennials margin of error is
±2.2 percentage points.

By Cindy Clark and Adrienne Lewis, USA TODAY

USA TODAY Snapshots®

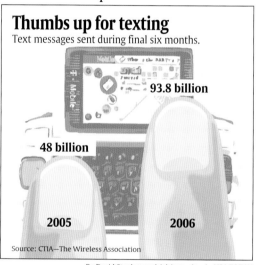

Thumbs up for texting

Text messages sent during final six months.

93.8 billion

48 billion

2005

2006

Source: CTIA—The Wireless Association

By David Stuckey and Adrienne Lewis, USA TODAY

279

USA TODAY Snapshots®

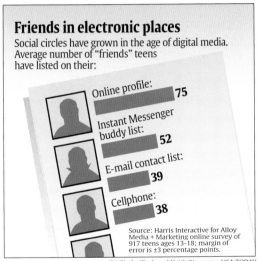

Friends in electronic places

Social circles have grown in the age of digital media. Average number of "friends" teens have listed on their:

Online profile: **75**

Instant Messenger buddy list: **52**

E-mail contact list: **39**

Cellphone: **38**

Source: Harris Interactive for Alloy Media + Marketing online survey of 917 teens ages 13-18; margin of error is ±3 percentage points.

By Cindy Clark and Keith Simmons, USA TODAY

USA TODAY Snapshots®

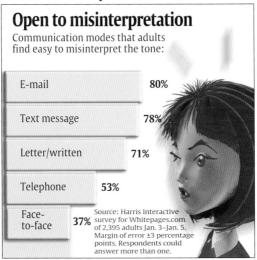

Open to misinterpretation

Communication modes that adults find easy to misinterpret the tone:

E-mail	80%
Text message	78%
Letter/written	71%
Telephone	53%
Face-to-face	37%

Source: Harris Interactive survey for Whitepages.com of 2,395 adults Jan. 3–Jan. 5. Margin of error ±3 percentage points. Respondents could answer more than one.

By Mary Cadden and Suzy Parker, USA TODAY

USA TODAY Snapshots®

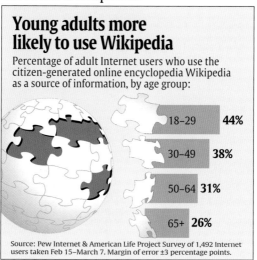

Young adults more likely to use Wikipedia

Percentage of adult Internet users who use the citizen-generated online encyclopedia Wikipedia as a source of information, by age group:

18–29 **44%**

30–49 **38%**

50–64 **31%**

65+ **26%**

Source: Pew Internet & American Life Project Survey of 1,492 Internet users taken Feb 15–March 7. Margin of error ±3 percentage points.

By Cindy Clark and Veronica Salazar, USA TODAY

USA TODAY Snapshots®

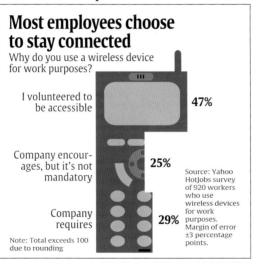

Most employees choose to stay connected

Why do you use a wireless device for work purposes?

I volunteered to be accessible **47%**

Company encourages, but it's not mandatory **25%**

Company requires **29%**

Note: Total exceeds 100 due to rounding

Source: Yahoo HotJobs survey of 920 workers who use wireless devices for work purposes. Margin of error ±3 percentage points.

By Jae Yang and Adrienne Lewis, USA TODAY

283

USA TODAY Snapshots®

Pets and the 'Net

Percentage of pet owners who use the Internet to obtain information about their pets:

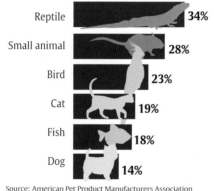

Reptile **34%**

Small animal **28%**

Bird **23%**

Cat **19%**

Fish **18%**

Dog **14%**

Source: American Pet Product Manufacturers Association

By David Stuckey and Robert W. Ahrens, USA TODAY

USA TODAY Snapshots®

Getting teen drivers to hang up

Percentage of teens who say the following could influence them to give up using cellphones while driving:

64%

58%

51%

License taken away if caught

Receive an insurance discount

Law against it

Source: Report by The Children's Hospital of Philadelphia and State Farm

By David Stuckey and Alejandro Gonzalez, USA TODAY

USA TODAY Snapshots®

Working remotely, vs. in the office

Do you think your work quality is perceived the same when you work remotely as when you are physically in the office?

Yes **55%**

No **45%**

Source: HotJobs survey of 1,465 workers. Margin of error: ±3 percentage points.

By Jae Yang and Karl Gelles, USA TODAY

USA TODAY Snapshots®

One e-mail address is not enough

How many personal e-mail addresses adult computer users regularly check:

One e-mail address **42%**

2 or 3 **48%**

4 or 5 **5%**

6 or more **5%**

Source: Ipsos for Habeas; Sept. 5–11 online survey of 2,347 adults. Margin of error ±2.1 percentage points.

By Cindy Clark and Alejandro Gonzalez, USA TODAY

USA TODAY Snapshots®

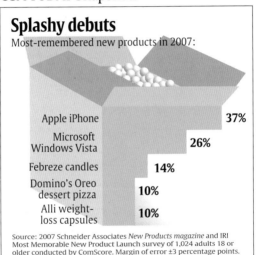

Splashy debuts
Most-remembered new products in 2007:

Product	%
Apple iPhone	37%
Microsoft Windows Vista	26%
Febreze candles	14%
Domino's Oreo dessert pizza	10%
Alli weight-loss capsules	10%

Source: 2007 Schneider Associates *New Products magazine* and IRI Most Memorable New Product Launch survey of 1,024 adults 18 or older conducted by ComScore. Margin of error ±3 percentage points.

By Jae Yang and Adrienne Lewis, USA TODAY

USA TODAY Snapshots®

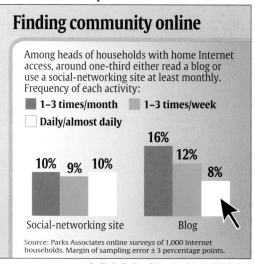

Finding community online

Among heads of households with home Internet access, around one-third either read a blog or use a social-networking site at least monthly. Frequency of each activity:

■ **1–3 times/month** ■ **1–3 times/week**
□ **Daily/almost daily**

10% **9%** **10%**
Social-networking site

16% **12%** **8%**
Blog

Source: Parks Associates online surveys of 1,000 Internet households. Margin of sampling error ± 3 percentage points.

By Cindy Clark and Veronica Salazar, USA TODAY

USA TODAY Snapshots®

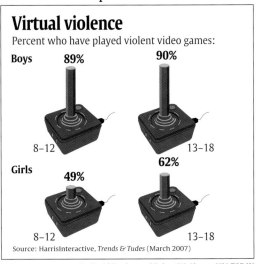

Virtual violence

Percent who have played violent video games:

Boys **89%** **90%**

8–12 13–18

Girls **62%**

49%

8–12 13–18

Source: HarrisInteractive, *Trends & Tudes* (March 2007)

By David Stuckey and Robert W. Ahrens, USA TODAY

USA TODAY Snapshots®

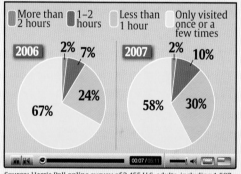

Tuning in to YouTube

Among U.S. adults who have ever watched a video on YouTube, 42% say they use the site frequently, up from 33% in 2006. Weekly use among YouTube viewers:

More than 2 hours   1–2 hours   Less than 1 hour   Only visited once or a few times

2006
2% 7%
24%
67%

2007
2% 10%
58% 30%

00:07 / 05:11

Source: Harris Poll online survey of 2,455 U.S. adults, including 1,587 YouTube viewers, conducted Nov. 7–13.

By Cindy Clark and Alejandro Gonzalez, USA TODAY

USA TODAY Snapshots®

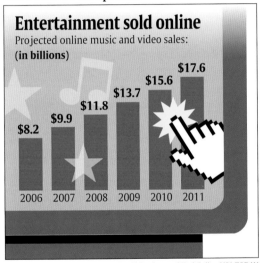

Entertainment sold online

Projected online music and video sales:

(in billions)

$8.2 — 2006
$9.9 — 2007
$11.8 — 2008
$13.7 — 2009
$15.6 — 2010
$17.6 — 2011

Source: Census Bureau   By David Stuckey and Karl Gelles, USA TODAY

USA TODAY Snapshots®

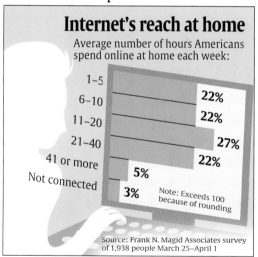

Internet's reach at home

Average number of hours Americans spend online at home each week:

1–5	22%
6–10	22%
11–20	27%
21–40	22%
41 or more	5%
Not connected	3%

Note: Exceeds 100 because of rounding

Source: Frank N. Magid Associates survey of 1,938 people March 25–April 1

By Anne R. Carey and Sam Ward, USA TODAY

USA TODAY Snapshots®

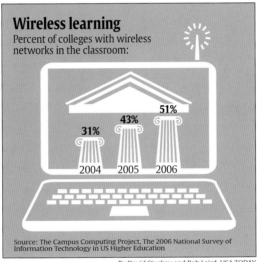

Wireless learning
Percent of colleges with wireless networks in the classroom:

31% 2004
43% 2005
51% 2006

Source: The Campus Computing Project, The 2006 National Survey of Information Technology in US Higher Education

By David Stuckey and Bob Laird, USA TODAY

USA TODAY Snapshots®

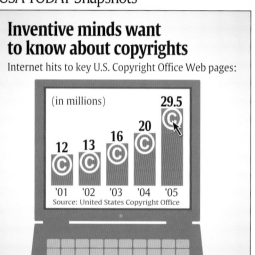

Inventive minds want to know about copyrights

Internet hits to key U.S. Copyright Office Web pages:

(in millions)

12	13	16	20	29.5
'01	'02	'03	'04	'05

Source: United States Copyright Office

By David Stuckey and Alejandro Gonzalez, USA TODAY

When you get dressed in the mornings before heading off to work, how much thought do you put into your selection? How many people believe that the way you dress affects your salary or your upward mobility? How much do you think that things over which you have no control—like your age—factor into your employment options? Do you see office discrimination as more or less of an issue today than in previous years?

Do you play a supervisory role in your workplace? What do workers say are their bosses' greatest sins? Would it surprise you to learn that arrogance is less of a problem than is trying to be everybody's friend? Are you happy in your current position? Were you passed over for a position you coveted? What mistakes have you made in a job interview? What are the most common job interview mistakes cited by employers?

How do you compare?

USA TODAY Snapshots®

Employers track personal e-mails

Most or all of employees' personal e-mail activities through personal accounts on work computers maybe captured and archived on company servers.

Percentage of the respondents who don't know certain e-mail activities are a business record:

Sent e-mails	43%
Received e-mails	55%
Created but unsent e-mails	66%

Source: WeComply 2006 Computer Use at Work survey of 1,000 workers. Margin of error ±3 percentage points.

By Jae Yang and Dave Merrill, USA TODAY

USA TODAY Snapshots®

Monitoring employees

Is it an invasion of privacy to monitor employees' e-mail and/or Internet use at work?

Yes
44%

Don't
know
8%

No
48%

Source: OPEN from American Express Small Business Monitor survey of 626 small-business owners and managers of companies with fewer than 100 employees. Margin of error ±4 percentage points.

By Jae Yang and Marcy E. Mullins, USA TODAY

USA TODAY Snapshots®

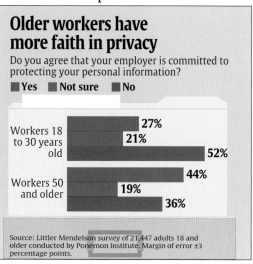

Older workers have more faith in privacy

Do you agree that your employer is committed to protecting your personal information?

■ Yes ■ Not sure ■ No

Workers 18 to 30 years old
- 27%
- 21%
- 52%

Workers 50 and older
- 44%
- 19%
- 36%

Source: Littler Mendelson survey of 21,447 adults 18 and older conducted by Ponemon Institute. Margin of error ±3 percentage points.

By Jae Yang and Adrienne Lewis, USA TODAY

USA TODAY Snapshots®

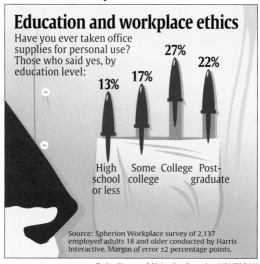

Education and workplace ethics

Have you ever taken office supplies for personal use? Those who said yes, by education level:

13% High school or less

17% Some college

27% College

22% Post-graduate

Source: Spherion Workplace survey of 2,137 employed adults 18 and older conducted by Harris Interactive. Margin of error ±2 percentage points.

By Jae Yang and Alejandro Gonzalez, USA TODAY

USA TODAY Snapshots®

Top workplace frustrations

Poor communication by senior management about the business	**17%**
General office politics	**16%**
Lack of teamwork	**15%**
Having to use politically correct language	**9%**
Nosy co-workers	**6%**

Source: Opinion Research survey of 1,198 workers.
Weighted to actual population proportion.

By Jae Yang and Sam Ward, USA TODAY

USA TODAY Snapshots®

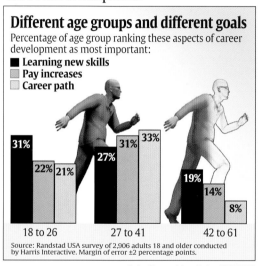

Different age groups and different goals

Percentage of age group ranking these aspects of career development as most important:

- ■ **Learning new skills**
- ▨ **Pay increases**
- □ **Career path**

18 to 26	31% 22% 21%
27 to 41	27% 31% 33%
42 to 61	19% 14% 8%

Source: Randstad USA survey of 2,906 adults 18 and older conducted by Harris Interactive. Margin of error ±2 percentage points.

By Jae Yang and Suzy Parker, USA TODAY

USA TODAY Snapshots®

Most common job interview mistakes noticed by employers

Little or no knowledge of the company — **47%**

Unprepared to discuss skills and experience — **17%**

Unprepared to discuss career plans and goals — **9%**

Limited enthusiasm — **9%**

Lack of eye contact — **3%**

Source: Accountemps study of 150 senior executives

By jae Yang and Adrienne Lewis, USA TODAY

USA TODAY Snapshots®

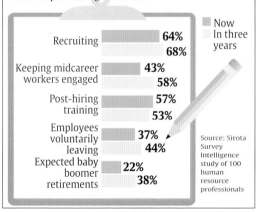

HR challenges

Top human resource challenges that are having the most impact on organizations:

	Now	In three years
Recruiting	64%	68%
Keeping midcareer workers engaged	43%	58%
Post-hiring training	57%	53%
Employees voluntarily leaving	37%	44%
Expected baby boomer retirements	22%	38%

Source: Sirota Survey Intelligence study of 100 human resource professionals

By Jae Yang and Adrienne Lewis, USA TODAY

USA TODAY Snapshots®

Longer résumés more acceptable

What is the preferable length of a résumé?

■ 2006
■ 1996

	2006	1996
One page	52%	73%
Two pages	44%	25%
Three or more	3%	1%

Source: Accountemps survey of 150 senior executives

By Jae Yang and Dave Merrill, USA TODAY

USA TODAY Snapshots®

Vacation days for job interviews

Have you ever used vacation days to interview for a new job?

Yes
31%

No
69%

Source: Yahoo HotJobs' Summer Vacation survey of 1,186 workers. Margin of error ±3 percentage points.

By Jae Yang and Bob Laird, USA TODAY

USA TODAY Snapshots®

Would your company hire a qualified 72-year-old CEO?

No
47%

Yes
53%

Source: CTParners
survey of 158
senior executives

By Jae Yang and Julie Snider, USA TODAY

USA TODAY Snapshots®

Dressing for success

Do you think how you dress at work affects your job, salary or promotions?

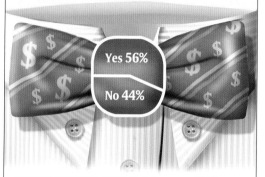

Yes 56%

No 44%

Source: Yahoo HotJobs Dress in the Workplace survey of 2,198 respondents. Margin of error ±3 percentage points.

By Jae Yang and Karl Gelles, USA TODAY

USA TODAY Snapshots®

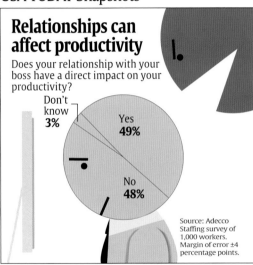

Relationships can affect productivity

Does your relationship with your boss have a direct impact on your productivity?

Don't know **3%**

Yes **49%**

No **48%**

Source: Adecco Staffing survey of 1,000 workers. Margin of error ±4 percentage points.

By Jae Yang and Adrienne Lewis, USA TODAY

USA TODAY Snapshots®

Employees want to make a difference

What do you think is the most important factor in job success? Top factors:

Using my talents to make a difference	36%
Financial success	29%
New opportunities	13%
Creating new solutions to existing problems	9%
Being able to give back to my community and society at large	9%

Source: Ace Hardware survey of 1,059 adults 18 and older conducted by Impulse Research. Margin of error ±3 percentage points.

By Jae Yang and Adrienne Lewis, USA TODAY

USA TODAY Snapshots®

Employees prefer not to relocate

If your company was acquired by another company, would you relocate to keep your job?

No
60%

Source: Principal Financial Group survey of 1,137 employees. Margin of error ±3 percentage points.

Yes
40%

By Jae Yang and Marcy E. Mullins, USA TODAY

USA TODAY Snapshots®

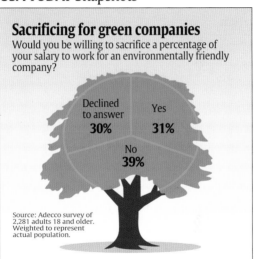

Sacrificing for green companies
Would you be willing to sacrifice a percentage of
your salary to work for an environmentally friendly
company?

Declined
to answer
30%

Yes
31%

No
39%

Source: Adecco survey of
2,281 adults 18 and older.
Weighted to represent
actual population.

By Jae Yang and Keith Simmons, USA TODAY

USA TODAY Snapshots®

Minorities more skeptical that promotions are based on merit

What is the most important quality for advancement in your workplace?

Job performance	Who you know	Seniority
Hispanic 57%	Hispanic 20%	Hispanic 12%
Black 58%	Black 13%	Black 15%
White 65%	White 20%	White 9%

Source: Novations Group survey of 688 employed Americans conducted by International Communications Research. Margin of error ±4 percentage points.

By Jae Yang and Keith Simmons, USA TODAY

USA TODAY Snapshots®

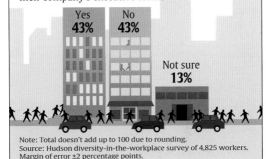

Employees split on workplace diversity

Seventy percent of survey respondents agree that having a diverse workforce is important. Do they think there is racial, ethnic and gender diversity in their company's executive team?

Yes
43%

No
43%

Not sure
13%

Note: Total doesn't add up to 100 due to rounding.
Source: Hudson diversity-in-the-workplace survey of 4,825 workers.
Margin of error ±2 percentage points.

By Jae Yang and Alejandro Gonzalez, USA TODAY

USA TODAY Snapshots®

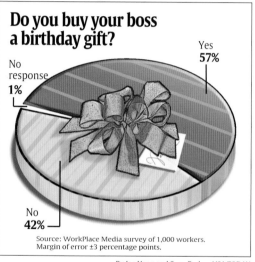

Do you buy your boss a birthday gift?

No response
1%

Yes
57%

No
42%

Source: WorkPlace Media survey of 1,000 workers.
Margin of error ±3 percentage points.

By Jae Yang and Suzy Parker, USA TODAY

USA TODAY Snapshots®

Older workers, younger bosses

Are you comfortable reporting to a manager who is younger than you?

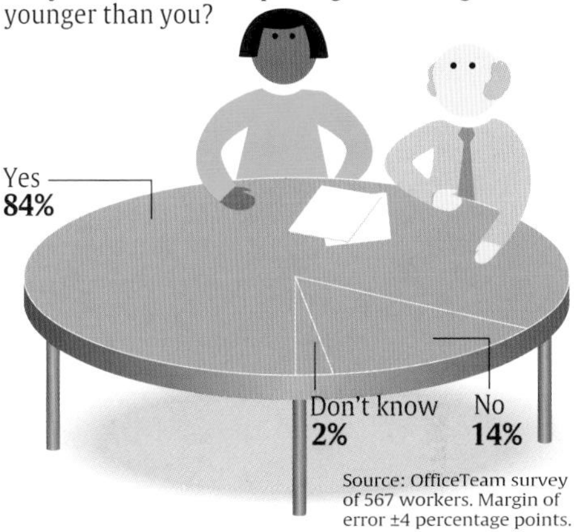

Yes
84%

Don't know
2%

No
14%

Source: OfficeTeam survey of 567 workers. Margin of error ±4 percentage points.

By Jae Yang and Adrienne Lewis, USA TODAY

USA TODAY Snapshots®

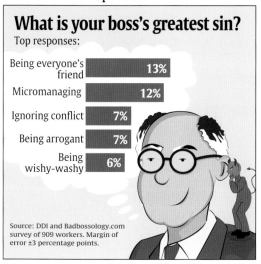

What is your boss's greatest sin?

Top responses:

Being everyone's friend	13%
Micromanaging	12%
Ignoring conflict	7%
Being arrogant	7%
Being wishy-washy	6%

Source: DDI and Badbossology.com survey of 909 workers. Margin of error ±3 percentage points.

By Jae Yang and Veronica Salazar, USA TODAY

USA TODAY Snapshots®

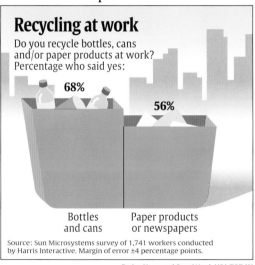

Recycling at work

Do you recycle bottles, cans and/or paper products at work? Percentage who said yes:

68%

56%

Bottles and cans

Paper products or newspapers

Source: Sun Microsystems survey of 1,741 workers conducted by Harris Interactive. Margin of error ±4 percentage points.

By Jae Yang and Sam Ward, USA TODAY

USA TODAY Snapshots®

Is it important for managers to have a sense of humor?

Yes
97%

No
3%

Source: Robert Half International survey of 492 workers. Margin of error ±4 percentage points.

By Jae Yang and Marcy E. Mullins, USA TODAY

320

USA TODAY Snapshots®

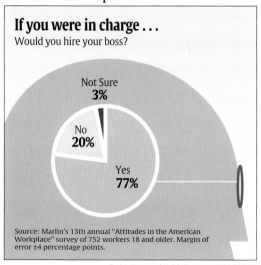

If you were in charge . . .
Would you hire your boss?

Not Sure
3%

No
20%

Yes
77%

Source: Marlin's 13th annual "Attitudes in the American Workplace" survey of 752 workers 18 and older. Margin of error ±4 percentage points.

By Jae Yang and Keith Simmons, USA TODAY

USA TODAY Snapshots®

Traits of good team players

What is the single-most-important characteristic of being a good team player? Top responses:

Meeting deadlines **40%**

Avoiding politics **25%**

Source:
Accountemps
survey of 150
senior executives.

Being pleasant to work with **20%**

Supporting managers **13%**

By Jae Yang and Keith Simmons, USA TODAY

USA TODAY Snapshots®

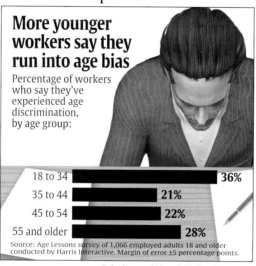

More younger workers say they run into age bias

Percentage of workers who say they've experienced age discrimination, by age group:

Age group	Percentage
18 to 34	36%
35 to 44	21%
45 to 54	22%
55 and older	28%

Source: Age Lessons survey of 1,066 employed adults 18 and older conducted by Harris Interactive. Margin of error ±5 percentage points.

By Jae Yang and Marcy E. Mullins, USA TODAY

USA TODAY Snapshots®

Paying the chiefs

Percentage of CEOs and employees who think CEOs are overpaid:

Employees **77%**

CEOs **64%**

Percentage who think CEOs are doing a good job:

CEOs **70%**

Employees **45%**

Source: BNET.com CEO Report Card survey of 136 CEOs and 1,318 employees. Margin of error ±3 percentage points.

By Jae Yang and Veronica Salazar, USA TODAY

USA TODAY Snapshots®

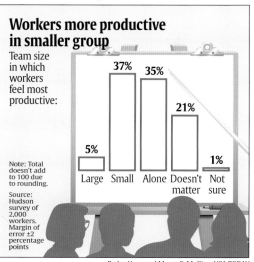

Workers more productive in smaller group

Team size in which workers feel most productive:

Large 5%
Small 37%
Alone 35%
Doesn't matter 21%
Not sure 1%

Note: Total doesn't add to 100 due to rounding.

Source: Hudson survey of 2,000 workers. Margin of error ±2 percentage points

By Jae Yang and Marcy E. Mullins, USA TODAY

USA TODAY Snapshots®

What employees want

What aspect is important when your employer communicates with you? Top responses:

Giving insights on how to be more effective — **52%**

Showing how to fit into the company's vision — **47%**

Explaining the company's vision — **45%**

Engaging on a personal level — **41%**

Note: Multiple responses allowed.

Source: Jack Morton Worldwide Experiential Marketing Global Consumer Response survey of 1,625 workers and job seekers conducted by Sponsorship Research International. Margin of error ±2 percentage points.

By Jae Yang and Marcy E. Mullins, USA TODAY

USA TODAY Snapshots®

Executives facing age discrimination

Age discrimination is a serious problem in today's executive employment market, say 63% of respondents. When does age become a significant factor in a hiring decision?

Before 45　**7%**
45 to 50　**27%**
51 to 55　**34%**
56 to 60　**18%**
After 60　**8%**
Never　**7%**

Source: Data compiled by ExecuNet. Margin of error ±2 percentage points.

By Jae Yang and Bob Laird USA TODAY

USA TODAY Snapshots®

Workplace design matters for most

Nine out of 10 respondents say better workplace design would make their company more competitive. Most desired improvement at workplace:

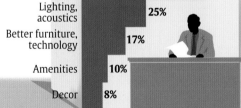

Organization/layout **49%**

Lighting, acoustics **25%**

Better furniture, technology **17%**

Amenities **10%**

Decor **8%**

Note: Multiple responses allowed.

Source: Gensler U.S. Workplace Survey 2006 of 2,013 workers conducted by D/R Added Value. Margin of error ±3 percentage points

By Jae Yang and Robert W. Ahrens, USA TODAY

USA TODAY Snapshots®

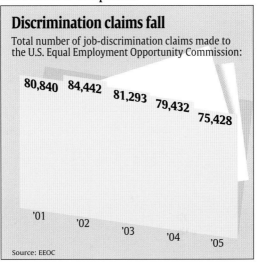

Discrimination claims fall

Total number of job-discrimination claims made to the U.S. Equal Employment Opportunity Commission:

80,840   84,442   81,293   79,432   75,428

'01   '02   '03   '04   '05

Source: EEOC

By David Stuckey and Adrienne Lewis, USA TODAY

USA TODAY Snapshots®

Who should be held legally responsible for corporate data security?

Board members
36%

Chief information security officer
42%

Chief executive officer
22%

Source: Circle study of 130 information technology executives

By Jae Yang and Suzy Parker, USA TODAY

USA TODAY Snapshots®

What is the most taboo topic to discuss at work?

Religion **29%**

Politics **14%**

Money **14%**

Office gossip **27%**

Personal life **16%**

Source: Adecco survey of 1,807 workers. Weighted to represent actual population.

By Jae Yang and Veronica Salazar, USA TODAY

USA TODAY Snapshots®

Most employers don't share company strategy

Of the companies with a formal strategy in place, 70% describe their performance as better than their competition, compared with 27% of those without it, according to a survey. Percentage of companies that tell their employees what the strategy is:

Don't tell
95%

Tell **5%**

Source: Cognos/Palladium Group "Making Strategy Execution a Competitive Advantage" study of 143 strategy management professionals

By Jae Yang and Alejandro Gonzalez, USA TODAY

USA TODAY Snapshots®

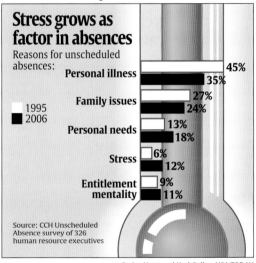

Stress grows as factor in absences

Reasons for unscheduled absences:

- 1995
- 2006

Personal illness	45% / 35%
Family issues	27% / 24%
Personal needs	13% / 18%
Stress	6% / 12%
Entitlement mentality	9% / 11%

Source: CCH Unscheduled Absence survey of 326 human resource executives

By Jae Yang and Karl Gelles, USA TODAY

USA TODAY Snapshots®

Women more cautious about workplace romance

Percentage of workers who think openly dating a co-worker would jeopardize their job security or advancement opportunities:

47%

36%

Women

Men

Source: 2007 Spherion Workplace Snapshot survey of 1,588 employed adults age 18 and older. Margin of error ±2 percentage points.

By Jae Yang and Marcy E. Mullins, USA TODAY

USA TODAY Snapshots®

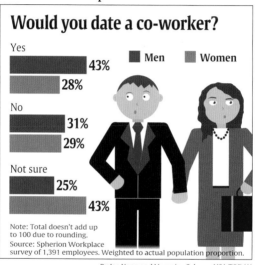

Would you date a co-worker?

Yes
- Men **43%**
- Women **28%**

No
- Men **31%**
- Women **29%**

Not sure
- Men **25%**
- Women **43%**

Note: Total doesn't add up to 100 due to rounding.
Source: Spherion Workplace survey of 1,391 employees. Weighted to actual population proportion.

By Jae Yang and Veronica Salazar, USA TODAY

USA TODAY Snapshots®

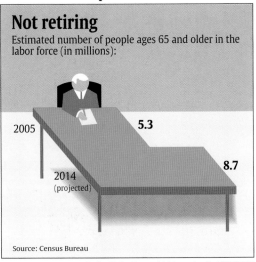

Not retiring

Estimated number of people ages 65 and older in the labor force (in millions):

2005   **5.3**

2014
(projected)

8.7

Source: Census Bureau

By David Stuckey and Adrienne Lewis, USA TODAY

USA TODAY Snapshots®

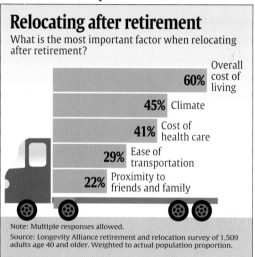

Relocating after retirement

What is the most important factor when relocating after retirement?

60% Overall cost of living

45% Climate

41% Cost of health care

29% Ease of transportation

22% Proximity to friends and family

Note: Multiple responses allowed.

Source: Longevity Alliance retirement and relocation survey of 1,509 adults age 40 and older. Weighted to actual population proportion.

By Jae Yang and Alejandro Gonzalez, USA TODAY

USA TODAY Snapshots®

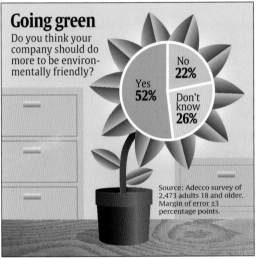

Going green

Do you think your company should do more to be environmentally friendly?

Yes **52%**

No **22%**

Don't know **26%**

Source: Adecco survey of 2,473 adults 18 and older. Margin of error ±3 percentage points.

By Jae Yang and Alejandro Gonzalez, USA TODAY

USA TODAY Snapshots®

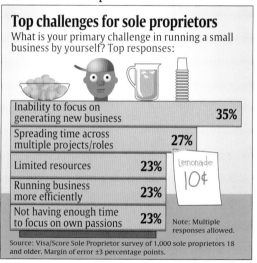

Top challenges for sole proprietors

What is your primary challenge in running a small business by yourself? Top responses:

Challenge	%
Inability to focus on generating new business	**35%**
Spreading time across multiple projects/roles	**27%**
Limited resources	**23%**
Running business more efficiently	**23%**
Not having enough time to focus on own passions	**23%**

Note: Multiple responses allowed.

Source: Visa/Score Sole Proprietor survey of 1,000 sole proprietors 18 and older. Margin of error ±3 percentage points.

By Jae Yang and Alejandro Gonzalez, USA TODAY

USA TODAY Snapshots®

Age drives midsize-company owners to cash out

What are the primary factors for selling your company? Top responses:

Age **57%**
Boredom/burnout **46%**
Liquidity/cash **45%**
Need for growth capital **37%**
Health **22%**

Note: Multiple responses allowed
Source: GW/Equity study of 200 midsize-company owners with annual revenues from $1 million to $150 million.

By Jae Yang and Alejandro Gonzalez, USA TODAY

USA TODAY Snapshots®

Majority of business owners start from scratch

How did you get your business? Top responses:

Started own business
52%

Purchased business from a non-family member
18%

Took over business from a family member
11%

Inherited family business
5%

Source: SunTrust study of 201 business owners with annual revenue of $10 million or more.

By Jae Yang and Alejandro Gonzalez, USA TODAY

▪ Education

Fewer students are electing to take the exams for admission to law school these days—what other trends are happening in education? What are colleges looking for in students' applications? Is the population more or less educated than it was twenty years ago? What states harbor the highest proportion of bachelor degree recipients?

Are you more likely to have scored well on your SATs if you're a math major or if you're an English major? Is your child more or less likely to participate in arts activities depending on your household income? What kind of student were you? Did you speak up in class? Or did you do just enough to get by?

Do you know the answer?

USA TODAY Snapshots®

Teachers' out-of-pocket expenses

Average amount of their own money teachers spend annually on classroom materials and supplies:

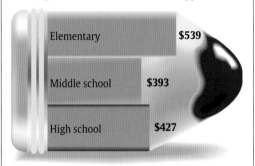

Elementary **$539**

Middle school **$393**

High school **$427**

Source: Quality Education Data Online Educator Panel representative sample of 957 teachers surveyed Sept. 26-29; margin of error is ±3 percentage points.

By Tracey Wong Briggs and Robert W. Ahrens, USA TODAY

USA TODAY Snapshots®

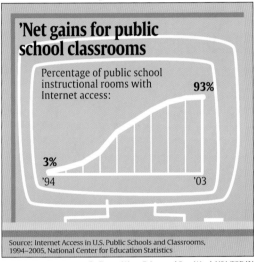

'Net gains for public school classrooms

Percentage of public school instructional rooms with Internet access:

93%

3%

'94   '03

Source: Internet Access in U.S. Public Schools and Classrooms, 1994–2005, National Center for Education Statistics

By Tracey Wong Briggs and Sam Ward, USA TODAY

USA TODAY Snapshots®

Threats to teachers

Number of teachers who reported that they were threatened with injury by a student in the previous 12 months:

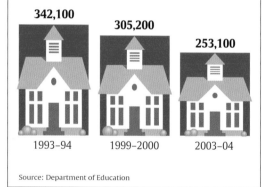

342,100 — 1993–94
305,200 — 1999–2000
253,100 — 2003–04

Source: Department of Education

By David Stuckey and Karl Gelles, USA TODAY

USA TODAY Snapshots®

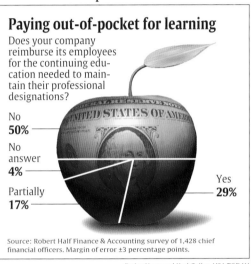

Paying out-of-pocket for learning

Does your company reimburse its employees for the continuing education needed to maintain their professional designations?

No
50%

No answer
4%

Partially
17%

Yes
29%

Source: Robert Half Finance & Accounting survey of 1,428 chief financial officers. Margin of error ±3 percentage points.

By Jae Yang and Karl Gelles, USA TODAY

USA TODAY Snapshots®

From campus to workplace

Nearly four out of five U.S. college seniors have started looking for a job, compared with three out of four around the world. Percentage of graduating seniors who have already found a job:

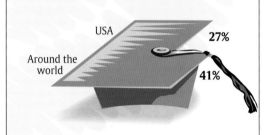

USA **27%**

Around the world **41%**

Source: Accenture College Senior survey of 407 U.S. graduating seniors and 2,057 graduating seniors around the world. Weighted to adjust for varied sample sizes

By Jae Yang and Robert W. Ahrens USA TODAY

USA TODAY Snapshots®

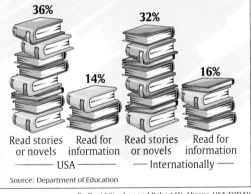

Global reading

Percentage of fourth-graders in the USA and internationally who said they read stories or novels or read for information every day or almost every day in 2006:

36%

32%

14%

16%

Read stories or novels · Read for information
— USA —

Read stories or novels · Read for information
— Internationally —

Source: Department of Education

By David Stuckey and Robert W. Ahrens, USA TODAY

USA TODAY Snapshots®

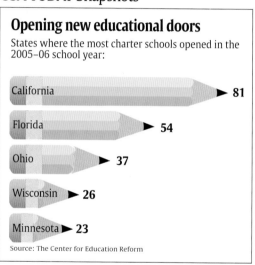

Opening new educational doors

States where the most charter schools opened in the 2005–06 school year:

California ➤ 81

Florida ➤ 54

Ohio ➤ 37

Wisconsin ➤ 26

Minnesota ➤ 23

Source: The Center for Education Reform

By David Stuckey and Adrienne Lewis, USA TODAY

USA TODAY Snapshots®

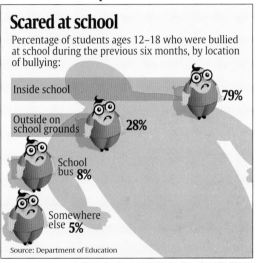

Scared at school

Percentage of students ages 12–18 who were bullied at school during the previous six months, by location of bullying:

Inside school **79%**

Outside on school grounds **28%**

School bus **8%**

Somewhere else **5%**

Source: Department of Education

By David Stuckey and Alejandro Gonzalez, USA TODAY

USA TODAY Snapshots®

Students let fingers do the calculating

Far more high school sophomores have used calculators (94%) than computers (39%) in math class. Percentage who report having used them with any frequency in math class:

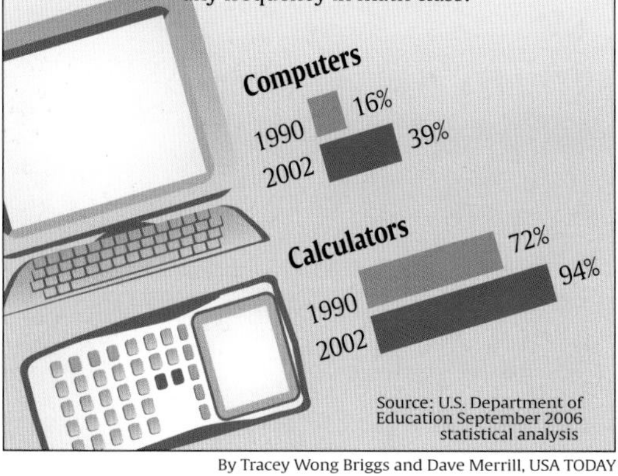

Computers

1990   16%

2002   39%

Calculators

1990   72%

2002   94%

Source: U.S. Department of Education September 2006 statistical analysis

By Tracey Wong Briggs and Dave Merrill, USA TODAY

352

USA TODAY Snapshots®

The lies have it

Overall, 42% of high school students think a person has to lie or cheat sometimes to succeed. By gender:

Male
50%

Female
33%

Source: Josephson Institute's 2006 Report Card on the Ethics of American Youth, a questionnaire survey of 36,000 high school students ages 14 to 19 from 114 schools, January–June. Margin of error is ±1 percentage point.

By Tracey Wong Briggs and Alejandro Gonzalez, USA TODAY

USA TODAY Snapshots®

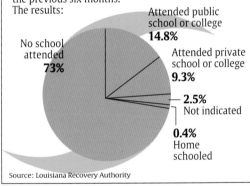

Katrina continues to ravage education

A survey conducted by the Louisiana Recovery Authority asked residents (ages 3 and older) of New Orleans to indicate their school attendance during the previous six months.
The results:

Attended public school or college
14.8%

No school attended
73%

Attended private school or college
9.3%

2.5%
Not indicated

0.4%
Home schooled

Source: Louisiana Recovery Authority

By David Stuckey and Sam Ward, USA TODAY

USA TODAY Snapshots®

Stopping improper materials

Percentage of public schools with procedures to prevent students from accessing inappropriate material on the Internet :

Monitoring by teachers or other staff

2001

91%

2005

96%

Blocking/ filtering software

2001

87%

2005

99%

Source: Department of Education

By David Stuckey and Robert W. Ahrens, USA TODAY

USA TODAY Snapshots®

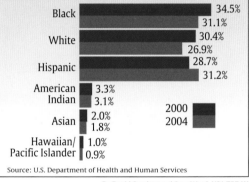

Head Start's changing demographics

The Head Start program, a comprehensive child development program aimed at low-income families, has seen its ethnic structure shift in recent years. The program's ethnic composition:

	2000	2004
Black	34.5%	31.1%
White	30.4%	26.9%
Hispanic	28.7%	31.2%
American Indian	3.3%	3.1%
Asian	2.0%	1.8%
Hawaiian/ Pacific Islander	1.0%	0.9%

Source: U.S. Department of Health and Human Services

By David Stuckey and Sam Ward, USA TODAY

USA TODAY Snapshots®

The East loves Latin

More than 135,000 students took the 30th annual National Latin Exam in 2007. States with the most exam takers:

State	Exam takers
Massachusetts	12,558
Virginia	11,503
New York	10,756
New Jersey	8,804
Pennsylvania	8,549
Texas	8,279

Source: National Latin Exam

By Tracey Wong Briggs and Bob Laird, USA TODAY

USA TODAY Snapshots®

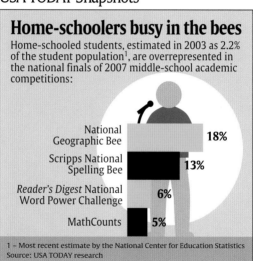

Home-schoolers busy in the bees

Home-schooled students, estimated in 2003 as 2.2% of the student population[1], are overrepresented in the national finals of 2007 middle-school academic competitions:

National Geographic Bee — **18%**

Scripps National Spelling Bee — **13%**

Reader's Digest National Word Power Challenge — **6%**

MathCounts — **5%**

1 – Most recent estimate by the National Center for Education Statistics
Source: USA TODAY research

By Tracey Wong Briggs and Sam Ward, USA TODAY

USA TODAY Snapshots®

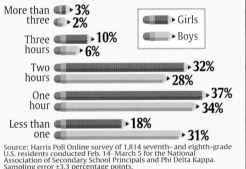

Middle-school homework gender gap

Middle-school girls say they spend an average of 1.4 hours a day on homework, compared with 1.1 hours for middle-school boys. The breakdown, by hours:

More than three ▸ **3%** ▸ **2%**

▸ Girls
▸ Boys

Three hours ▸ **10%** ▸ **6%**

Two hours ▸ **32%** ▸ **28%**

One hour ▸ **37%** ▸ **34%**

Less than one ▸ **18%** ▸ **31%**

Source: Harris Poll Online survey of 1,814 seventh- and eighth-grade U.S. residents conducted Feb. 14–March 5 for the National Association of Secondary School Principals and Phi Delta Kappa. Sampling error ±3.3 percentage points.

By Tracey Wong Briggs and Alejandro Gonzalez, USA TODAY

USA TODAY Snapshots®

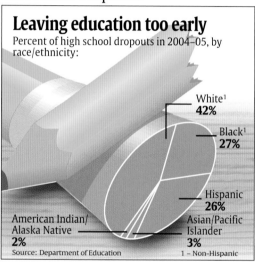

Leaving education too early

Percent of high school dropouts in 2004–05, by race/ethnicity:

White[1]
42%

Black[1]
27%

Hispanic
26%

Asian/Pacific
Islander
3%

American Indian/
Alaska Native
2%

Source: Department of Education

1 – Non-Hispanic

By David Stuckey and Marcy E. Mullins, USA TODAY

USA TODAY Snapshots®

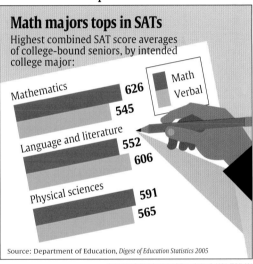

Math majors tops in SATs

Highest combined SAT score averages of college-bound seniors, by intended college major:

Math
Verbal

Mathematics **626**
545

Language and literature **552**
606

Physical sciences **591**
565

Source: Department of Education, *Digest of Education Statistics 2005*

By David Stuckey and Sam Ward, USA TODAY

USA TODAY Snapshots®

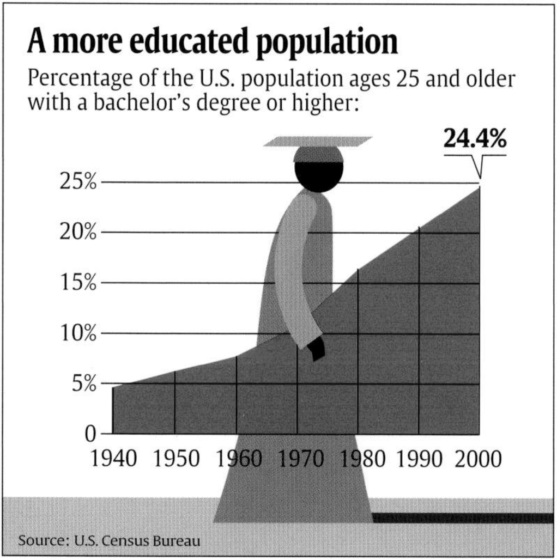

A more educated population
Percentage of the U.S. population ages 25 and older with a bachelor's degree or higher:
24.4%
25%
20%
15%
10%
5%
0
1940 1950 1960 1970 1980 1990 2000
Source: U.S. Census Bureau

By Tracey Wong Briggs and Sam Ward, USA TODAY

USA TODAY Snapshots®

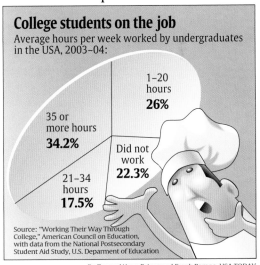

College students on the job

Average hours per week worked by undergraduates in the USA, 2003–04:

1–20 hours
26%

35 or more hours
34.2%

Did not work
22.3%

21–34 hours
17.5%

Source: "Working Their Way Through College," American Council on Education, with data from the National Postsecondary Student Aid Study, U.S. Department of Education

By Tracey Wong Briggs and Frank Pompa, USA TODAY

USA TODAY Snapshots®

The capital of higher learning

Places where the population, ages 25 and older, had the highest proportion with a bachelor's degree or higher in 2004:

45.7% — District of Columbia

36.7% — Mass.

35.5% — Colorado

35.4% — New Hampshire

35.2% — Maryland

Source: Census Bureau

By David Stuckey and Alejandro Gonzalez, USA TODAY

USA TODAY Snapshots®

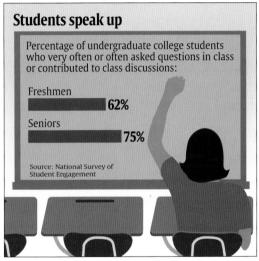

Students speak up

Percentage of undergraduate college students who very often or often asked questions in class or contributed to class discussions:

Freshmen
62%

Seniors
75%

Source: National Survey of Student Engagement

By David Stuckey and Alejandro Gonzalez, USA TODAY

USA TODAY Snapshots®

Talking students' heads off

Although male and female college faculty members spend about the same amount of time testing, men spend almost half of their class time lecturing. Percentage of time spent lecturing:

46%

35%

Men

Women

Source: National Survey of Student Engagement

By David Stuckey and Alejandro Gonzalez, USA TODAY

USA TODAY Snapshots®

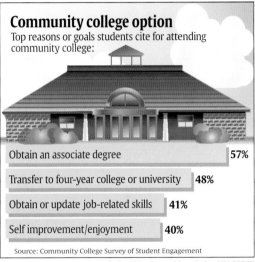

Community college option

Top reasons or goals students cite for attending community college:

Obtain an associate degree — **57%**

Transfer to four-year college or university — **48%**

Obtain or update job-related skills — **41%**

Self improvement/enjoyment — **40%**

Source: Community College Survey of Student Engagement

By David Stuckey and Suzy Parker, USA TODAY

USA TODAY Snapshots®

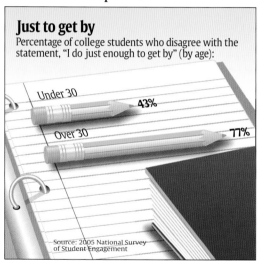

Just to get by

Percentage of college students who disagree with the statement, "I do just enough to get by" (by age):

Under 30 — 43%

Over 30 — 77%

Source: 2005 National Survey of Student Engagement

By David Stuckey and Marcy E. Mullins, USA TODAY

USA TODAY Snapshots®

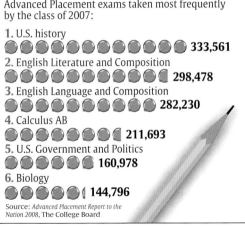

AP exams with the most takers

Advanced Placement exams taken most frequently by the class of 2007:

1. U.S. history
333,561

2. English Literature and Composition
298,478

3. English Language and Composition
282,230

4. Calculus AB
211,693

5. U.S. Government and Politics
160,978

6. Biology
144,796

Source: *Advanced Placement Report to the Nation 2008*, The College Board

By Michelle Healy and Julie Snider, USA TODAY

USA TODAY Snapshots®

More education means less time for TV but not for people

Average hours spent each weekday on these leisure activities, by educational attainment:

Less than a high school diploma   **Bachelor's degree or higher**

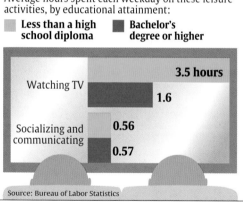

Watching TV **3.5 hours** / **1.6**

Socializing and communicating **0.56** / **0.57**

Source: Bureau of Labor Statistics

By David Stuckey and Adrienne Lewis, USA TODAY

USA TODAY Snapshots®

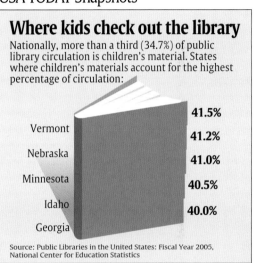

Where kids check out the library

Nationally, more than a third (34.7%) of public library circulation is children's material. States where children's materials account for the highest percentage of circulation:

State	Percentage
Vermont	41.5%
Nebraska	41.2%
Minnesota	41.0%
Idaho	40.5%
Georgia	40.0%

Source: Public Libraries in the United States: Fiscal Year 2005, National Center for Education Statistics

By Tracey Wong Briggs and Adrienne Lewis, USA TODAY

USA TODAY Snapshots®

What colleges look for

Percent of colleges reporting that these factors were of "considerable importance" to admit a student:

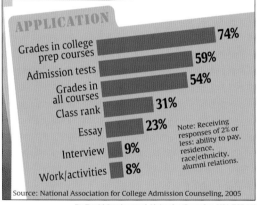

APPLICATION

Grades in college prep courses — 74%

Admission tests — 59%

Grades in all courses — 54%

Class rank — 31%

Essay — 23%

Interview — 9%

Work/activities — 8%

Note: Receiving responses of 2% or less: ability to pay, residence, race/ethnicity, alumni relations.

Source: National Association for College Admission Counseling, 2005

By David Stuckey and Alejandro Gonzalez, USA TODAY

USA TODAY Snapshots®

Tribal teaching

Asked how much they know about the history of their tribe or group, self-identified American Indian/Alaska Native eighth-graders said:

Some **54%**

Nothing or not much **14%**

A lot **32%**

Source: National Center for Education Statistics, 2007 National Indian Education Study

By Michelle Healy and Robert W. Ahrens, USA TODAY

USA TODAY Snapshots®

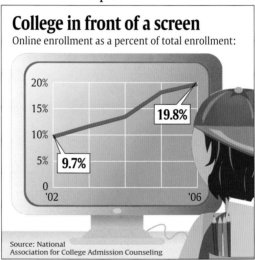

College in front of a screen

Online enrollment as a percent of total enrollment:

20%
15%
10%
5%
0

19.8%

9.7%

'02   '06

Source: National
Association for College Admission Counseling

By David Stuckey and Veronica Salazar, USA TODAY

USA TODAY Snapshots®

Dropping out late in game

Highest and lowest 12th-grade drop-out rates reported by states[1] during 2004-05 school year:

Highest
Alaska **10.3%**

Lowest
Connecticut **1.9%**

USA **4.9%**

1 — No data was available for Oregon

Note: No data was available for Oregon.
Source: National Center for Education Statistics

By David Stuckey and Alejandro Gonzalez, USA TODAY

USA TODAY Snapshots®

Sizing up private universities

Private, non-profit colleges and universities with the largest single-campus enrollment[1]:

New York University, New York City
40,004

Brigham Young University, Provo, Utah
34,067

University of Southern California, Los Angeles
32,836

Boston University
30,957

Harvard University, Cambridge, Mass.
25,017

George Washington University, Washington, D.C.
24,099

1 – Data are from fall 2005.
Source: American Council on Education, data from the U.S. Department of Education

By Tracy Wong Briggs and Karl Gelles, USA TODAY

USA TODAY Snapshots®

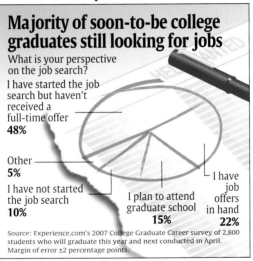

Majority of soon-to-be college graduates still looking for jobs

What is your perspective on the job search?

I have started the job search but haven't received a full-time offer
48%

Other
5%

I have not started the job search
10%

I plan to attend graduate school
15%

I have job offers in hand
22%

Source: Experience.com's 2007 College Graduate Career survey of 2,800 students who will graduate this year and next conducted in April. Margin of error ±2 percentage points.

By Jae Yang and Marcy E. Mullins, USA TODAY

USA TODAY Snapshots®

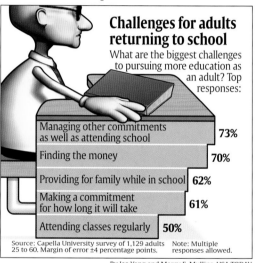

Challenges for adults returning to school

What are the biggest challenges to pursuing more education as an adult? Top responses:

Managing other commitments as well as attending school	73%
Finding the money	70%
Providing for family while in school	62%
Making a commitment for how long it will take	61%
Attending classes regularly	50%

Source: Capella University survey of 1,129 adults 25 to 60. Margin of error ±4 percentage points. Note: Multiple responses allowed.

By Jae Yang and Marcy E. Mullins, USA TODAY

USA TODAY Snapshots®

Helping them get a job

Services that MBA students are most likely to receive from their schools' career services offices:

Listings of current job openings	**71%**
Access to alumni network	**64%**
Post-graduate placement assistance	**61%**
Career counseling/coaching sessions	**61%**
Online resources	**60%**

Source: Graduate Management Admission Council, Global MBA Graduate Survey 2006

By David Stuckey and Alejandro Gonzalez, USA TODAY

USA TODAY Snapshots®

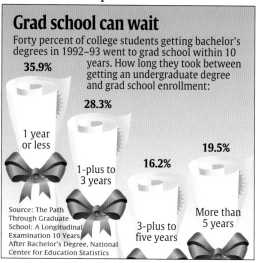

Grad school can wait

Forty percent of college students getting bachelor's degrees in 1992–93 went to grad school within 10 years. How long they took between getting an undergraduate degree and grad school enrollment:

35.9%

28.3%

19.5%

16.2%

1 year or less

1-plus to 3 years

3-plus to five years

More than 5 years

Source: The Path Through Graduate School: A Longitudinal Examination 10 Years After Bachelor's Degree, National Center for Education Statistics

By Tracey Wong Briggs and Marcy E. Mullins, USA TODAY

USA TODAY Snapshots®

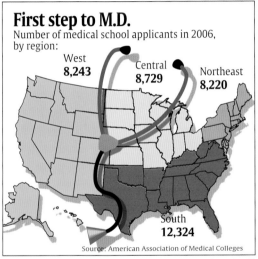

First step to M.D.
Number of medical school applicants in 2006,
by region:

West
8,243

Central
8,729

Northeast
8,220

South
12,324

Source: American Association of Medical Colleges

By David Stuckey and Sam Ward, USA TODAY

USA TODAY Snapshots®

Med schools gain female students, faculty

- % female med school graduates
- % female med school faculty[1]

47%

29%

7% 7%

50
40
30
20
10
0

1965   2005

1 — Full-time faculty with
U.S. medical degrees
Source: Association of
American Medical Colleges

By Tracey Wong Briggs and Bob Laird, USA TODAY

USA TODAY Snapshots®

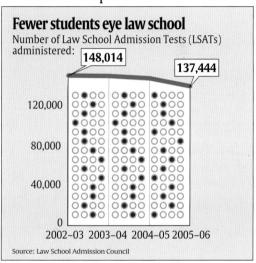

Fewer students eye law school
Number of Law School Admission Tests (LSATs)
administered:

148,014

137,444

120,000

80,000

40,000

0

2002–03 2003–04 2004–05 2005–06

Source: Law School Admission Council

By David Stuckey and Adrienne Lewis, USA TODAY

USA TODAY Snapshots®

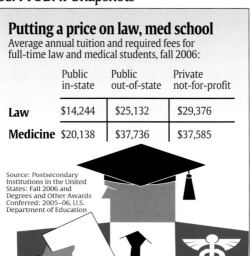

Putting a price on law, med school

Average annual tuition and required fees for full-time law and medical students, fall 2006:

	Public in-state	Public out-of-state	Private not-for-profit
Law	$14,244	$25,132	$29,376
Medicine	$20,138	$37,736	$37,585

Source: Postsecondary Institutions in the United States: Fall 2006 and Degrees and Other Awards Conferred: 2005–06, U.S. Department of Education

By Tracey Wong Briggs and Keith Simmons, USA TODAY

USA TODAY Snapshots®

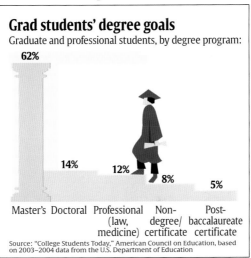

Grad students' degree goals

Graduate and professional students, by degree program:

62% Master's

14% Doctoral

12% Professional (law, medicine)

8% Non-degree/ certificate

5% Post-baccalaureate certificate

Source: "College Students Today," American Council on Education, based on 2003–2004 data from the U.S. Department of Education

By Mary Katherine Bartholomew and Robert W. Ahrens, USA TODAY

USA TODAY Snapshots®

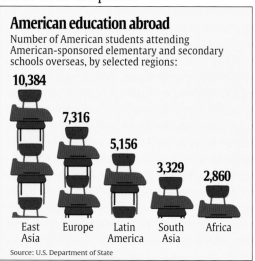

American education abroad

Number of American students attending American-sponsored elementary and secondary schools overseas, by selected regions:

10,384 — East Asia
7,316 — Europe
5,156 — Latin America
3,329 — South Asia
2,860 — Africa

Source: U.S. Department of State

By David Stuckey and Alejandro Gonzalez, USA TODAY

USA TODAY Snapshots®

More women go to grad school

As graduate school enrollment has risen, so has the proportion of female graduate students. Enrollment in thousands:

━━━ Men
━━━ Women

- 675
- 670
- 1,309
- 877

1,400
700

'80   '85   '90   '95   '00   '05

Source: Mini-Digest of Education Statistics 2006, U.S. Department of Education

By Tracey Wong Briggs and Alejandro Gonzalez, USA TODAY

■ Sports

What kind of sporting goods have you purchased lately? With equipment sales close to $24 billion in past years, what is everyone else spending his or her money on? Golfing? Fishing? Camping? Do you watch sports on television? How often do you see professional games in person? What sports garner the most spectators?

Do you participate in March Madness office pools? How much do you put in the pot? What's the average? Do you play virtual sports—at home or online? What game is your neighbor most likely playing at home? What sports are kids most likely to play at school? Do you wear your team loyalty on your sleeve?

What's your position?

USA TODAY Snapshots®

Splurging on favorite sports

Sporting goods equipment sales reached almost $24 billion in 2005. Sports/recreational activities on which consumers spent the most money for equipment in 2005 (in billions):

Exercise **$5.2**

Golf **$3.5**

Hunting and firearms **$3.4**

Fishing tackle **$2.1**

Camping **$1.4**

Source: National Sporting Goods Association

By Ellen J. Horrow and Bob Laird, USA TODAY

USA TODAY Snapshots®

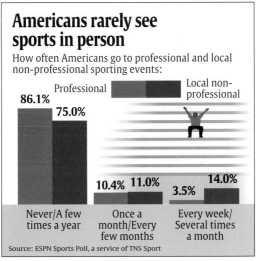

Americans rarely see sports in person

How often Americans go to professional and local non-professional sporting events:

Professional — Local non-professional

86.1%
75.0%

10.4% 11.0%
3.5%
14.0%

| Never/A few times a year | Once a month/Every few months | Every week/Several times a month |

Source: ESPN Sports Poll, a service of TNS Sport

By Ellen J. Horrow and Sam Ward, USA TODAY

USA TODAY Snapshots®

U.S. fans show support for World Cup

Soccer may not be the most popular sport in the USA, but Americans did turn out to see the World Cup when it was last played in the USA. World Cup tournaments with the highest average attendance:

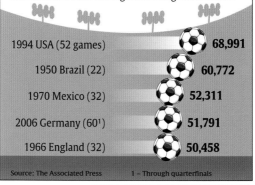

1994 USA (52 games)	68,991
1950 Brazil (22)	60,772
1970 Mexico (32)	52,311
2006 Germany (60[1])	51,791
1966 England (32)	50,458

Source: The Associated Press   1 – Through quarterfinals

By Ellen J. Horrow and Adrienne Lewis, USA TODAY

USA TODAY Snapshots®

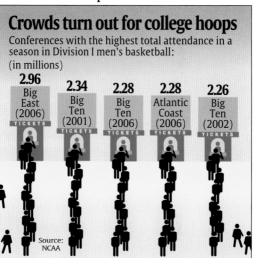

Crowds turn out for college hoops

Conferences with the highest total attendance in a season in Division I men's basketball:
(in millions)

2.96 Big East (2006)

2.34 Big Ten (2001)

2.28 Big Ten (2006)

2.28 Atlantic Coast (2006)

2.26 Big Ten (2002)

Source: NCAA

By Ellen J. Horrow and Alejandro Gonzalez, USA TODAY

USA TODAY Snapshots®

Best after the bye

NFL teams began getting a break this week as the league's bye weeks began. Teams with the best records after having the previous week off (since 1990):

Minnesota, 15-4	**.789**
Philadelphia 15-4	**.789**
Denver 15-4	**.789**
Dallas 14-5	**.737**
Buffalo 13-6	**.684**

Source: NFL

By Matt Young and Alejandro Gonzalez, USA TODAY

USA TODAY Snapshots®

March Madness at work

Almost 70% of working Americans are not participating in March Madness basketball pools. Of the 30% who are, most will likely put $10 or less into the pot. How working Americans keep up with the games:

Watch games at home only
33%

Keep track of games online
10%

Watch games at work and at home
4%

Watch games during work hours
1%

5% Other

47%
Have no interest in the tournament

Source: WorkPlace Media   By Ellen J. Horrow and Sam Ward, USA TODAY

395

USA TODAY Snapshots®

Most popular high school girls' sports

The number of girls participating in high school sports exceeded 3 million for the first time, with 3,021,807 in the 2006–07 school year. Sports with the largest participation (by number of schools):

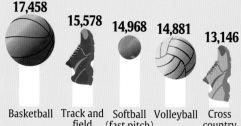

| 17,458 | 15,578 | 14,968 | 14,881 | 13,146 |
| Basketball | Track and field (outdoor) | Softball (fast pitch) | Volleyball | Cross country |

Source: National Federation of State High School Associations

By Ellen J. Horrow and Alejandro Gonzalez, USA TODAY

USA TODAY Snapshots®

What needs work with the golf game

What golf students need the most help with, according to PGA certified professionals[1]:

Short-game shots
65%

Approach and swing
22%

Driver shots
9%

4% Putting

1 – Survey conducted among PGA members who are graduates of the Certified Professional Program.

Source: PGA of America   By Ellen J. Horrow and Sam Ward, USA TODAY

USA TODAY Snapshots®

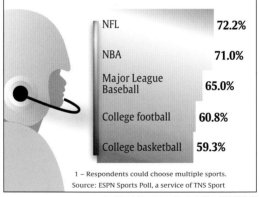

NFL, NBA top kids' list

Sports kids 7–11 watch on television the most[1]:

NFL **72.2%**

NBA **71.0%**

Major League Baseball **65.0%**

College football **60.8%**

College basketball **59.3%**

1 – Respondents could choose multiple sports.
Source: ESPN Sports Poll, a service of TNS Sport

By Ellen J. Horrow and Julie Snider, USA TODAY

USA TODAY Snapshots®

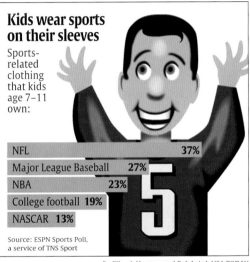

Kids wear sports on their sleeves

Sports-related clothing that kids age 7–11 own:

NFL	37%
Major League Baseball	27%
NBA	23%
College football	19%
NASCAR	13%

Source: ESPN Sports Poll, a service of TNS Sport

By Ellen J. Horrow and Bob Laird, USA TODAY

USA TODAY Snapshots®

Longest MLB losing season streaks

Pittsburgh, which hasn't had a winning season since the first Clinton administration, extended its streak of losing seasons in 2008:

Pittsburgh **16**

Baltimore **11**

Cincinnati **8**

Kansas City **5**

Source: USA TODAY research

By Matt Young and Sam Ward, USA TODAY

USA TODAY Snapshots®

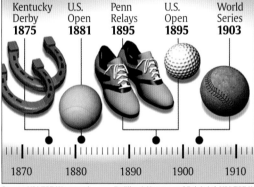

Competing for more than a century
One of track and field's biggest and oldest events, the Penn Relays, takes place annually in Philadelphia. Some of the oldest sporting events held in the USA:

Kentucky Derby	U.S. Open	Penn Relays	U.S. Open	World Series
1875	**1881**	**1895**	**1895**	**1903**

| 1870 | 1880 | 1890 | 1900 | 1910 |

Source: USA TODAY research   By Ellen J. Horrow and Bob Laird, USA TODAY

USA TODAY Snapshots®

Preakness winners provide big payday

Preakness champion Bernardini paid $27.80 to win, the eighth-largest win payoff in the race's history. Highest payoffs to win in the Preakness:

Master Derby (1975) — $48.80

Coventry (1925) — $45.60

Display (1926) — $40.70

Bee Bee Bee (1972) — $39.40

Source: Pimlico media guide

By Ellen J. Horrow and Marcy E. Mullins, USA TODAY

USA TODAY Snapshots®

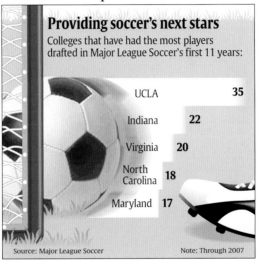

Providing soccer's next stars

Colleges that have had the most players drafted in Major League Soccer's first 11 years:

UCLA	35
Indiana	22
Virginia	20
North Carolina	18
Maryland	17

Source: Major League Soccer   Note: Through 2007

By Ellen J. Horrow and Marcy E. Mullins, USA TODAY

USA TODAY Snapshots®

Car companies get set to race

Car manufacturers with the most entries in the NOPI Drag Racing Association opener in 2006.

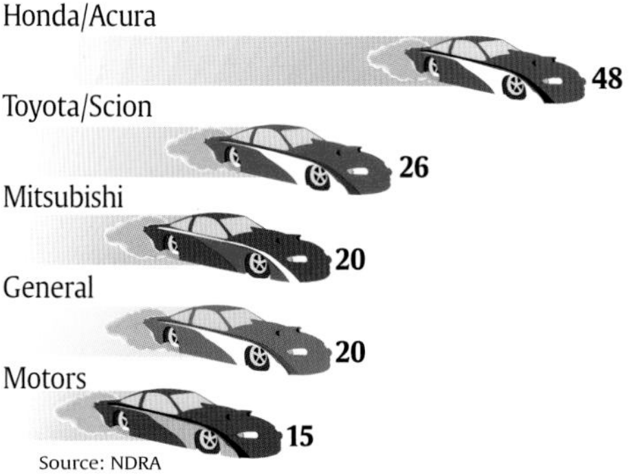

Honda/Acura **48**

Toyota/Scion **26**

Mitsubishi **20**

General **20**

Motors **15**

Source: NDRA

By Ellen J. Horrow and Robert W. Ahrens, USA TODAY

404

USA TODAY Snapshots®

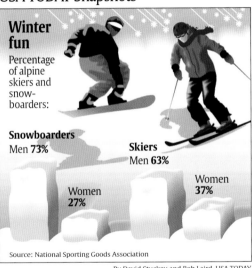

Winter fun

Percentage of alpine skiers and snowboarders:

Snowboarders
Men **73%**

Women **27%**

Skiers
Men **63%**

Women **37%**

Source: National Sporting Goods Association

By David Stuckey and Bob Laird, USA TODAY

USA TODAY Snapshots®

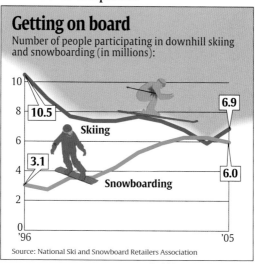

Getting on board

Number of people participating in downhill skiing and snowboarding (in millions):

10.5

Skiing

3.1

Snowboarding

6.9

6.0

'96   '05

Source: National Ski and Snowboard Retailers Association

By Adrienne Lewis, USA TODAY

406

USA TODAY Snapshots®

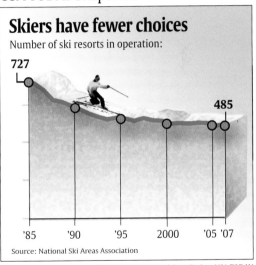

Skiers have fewer choices

Number of ski resorts in operation:

727

485

'85   '90   '95   2000   '05 '07

Source: National Ski Areas Association

By David Stuckey and Suzy Parker, USA TODAY

USA TODAY Snapshots®

Americans wear loyalty on their sleeve
More than 43% of American sports fans own clothing with professional team logos on it. Teams whose clothing Americans own:

Dallas Cowboys — 10.6%
New York Yankees — 8.0%
Green Bay Packers — 7.7%
Pittsburgh Steelers — 7.3%
Oakland Raiders — 5.9%

Source: ESPN Sports Poll, a service of TNS Sport

By Ellen J. Horrow and Alejandro Gonzalez, USA TODAY

USA TODAY Snapshots®

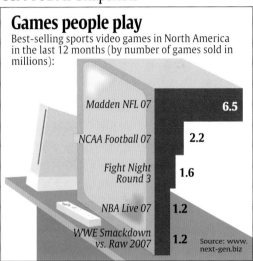

Games people play

Best-selling sports video games in North America in the last 12 months (by number of games sold in millions):

Madden NFL 07	6.5
NCAA Football 07	2.2
Fight Night Round 3	1.6
NBA Live 07	1.2
WWE Smackdown vs. Raw 2007	1.2

Source: www.next-gen.biz

By Ellen J. Horrow and Adrienne Lewis, USA TODAY

USA TODAY Snapshots®

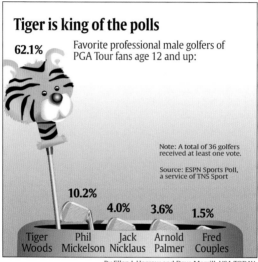

Tiger is king of the polls

Favorite professional male golfers of PGA Tour fans age 12 and up:

62.1%

Note: A total of 36 golfers received at least one vote.

Source: ESPN Sports Poll, a service of TNS Sport

Tiger Woods	Phil Mickelson	Jack Nicklaus	Arnold Palmer	Fred Couples
62.1%	10.2%	4.0%	3.6%	1.5%

By Ellen J. Horrow and Dave Merrill, USA TODAY

USA TODAY Snapshots®

Where crowds gather for tennis
Largest tennis stadiums by seating capacity:

Arthur Ashe Stadium (US Open)	**23,226**
Indian Wells Tennis Garden (Pacific Life Open)	**16,100**
Court Phillipe Chatrier (French Open)	**15,109**
All England Club (Wimbledon)	**15,000**
Qi Zhong Stadium (Tennis Masters Cup)	**15,000**
Rod Laver Arena (Australian Open)	**15,000**

Source: Pacific Life Ocean

By Ellen J. Horrow and Adrienne Lewis, USA TODAY

USA TODAY Snapshots®

Tennis participation on the rise

The number of Americans who play tennis has increased 8.2% since 2001, and the 25 million who currently play is the highest in 15 years. Tennis participation in the USA (in millions):

2001

2003   **23.2**

   23.9

2005   **24.7**

2007   **25.1**

Source: United States Tennis Association

By Ellen J. Horrow and Adrienne Lewis, USA TODAY

USA TODAY Snapshots®

Top sky routes of America

Number of airline passengers from December 2006 to November 2007 (in millions):

New York City–Chicago	3.47
Washington–Chicago	2.82
Atlanta–Orlando	2.77
Los Angeles–Chicago	2.71
Atlanta–New York City	2.69

Source: Bureau of Transportation Statistics

Note: Routes go in both directions.

By David Stuckey and Suzy Parker, USA TODAY

USA TODAY Snapshots®

Kansas tops in conference titles

Most regular-season conference titles
(includes shared or divisional titles)[1]:

Kansas (Missouri Valley, Big 8, Big 12)	50
Kentucky (Southern, Southeastern)	49
Pennsylvania (Ivy)	37
North Carolina (Southern, Atlantic Coast)	32

1 – Through 2006–07

Source: NCAA

By Ellen J. Horrow and Suzy Parker, USA TODAY

USA TODAY Snapshots®

Canadian Cup drought

Not since the Montreal Canadiens in 1993 has a team from Canada won the Stanley Cup, the oldest professional sports trophy in North America. Longest droughts between Stanley Cups for Canadian teams:

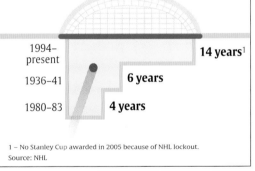

1994–present   **14 years**[1]

1936–41   **6 years**

1980–83   **4 years**

1 – No Stanley Cup awarded in 2005 because of NHL lockout.

Source: NHL

By Kevin Greer and Adrienne Lewis, USA TODAY

USA TODAY Snapshots®

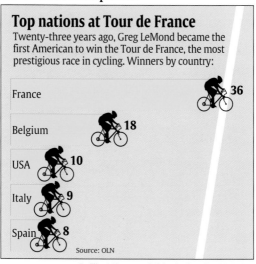

Top nations at Tour de France

Twenty-three years ago, Greg LeMond became the first American to win the Tour de France, the most prestigious race in cycling. Winners by country:

Country	Winners
France	36
Belgium	18
USA	10
Italy	9
Spain	8

Source: OLN

By Ellen J. Horrow and Alejandro Gonzalez, USA TODAY

USA TODAY Snapshots®

Starting on a winning note

The Major League Baseball season officially opens today. Franchises with the most wins on opening day:

Chicago Cubs

73

San Francisco Giants[1]

69

Pittsburgh Pirates

64

Atlanta Braves[2]

63

1 – Includes games won as New York Giants.
2 – Includes games won as Boston Braves and Milwaukee Braves.

Source: Elias Sports Bureau

By Ellen J. Horrow and Adrienne Lewis, USA TODAY

USA TODAY Snapshots®

Photo finishes in Texas

Smallest winning margins in the Nationwide Series races at Texas (winner in parentheses):

	Second
2007 O'Reilly 300 (Matt Kenseth)	0.128
1998 Coca-Cola 300 (Dale Earnhardt Jr.)	0.178
2001 Jani-King 300 (Kevin Harvick)	0.246
2006 O'Reilly 300 (Kurt Busch)	0.265
2005 O'Reilly 300 (Kasey Kahne)	0.304

Source: Texas Motor Speedway

By Ellen J. Horrow and Alejandro Gonzalez, USA TODAY

USA TODAY Snapshots®

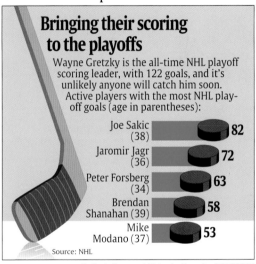

Bringing their scoring to the playoffs

Wayne Gretzky is the all-time NHL playoff scoring leader, with 122 goals, and it's unlikely anyone will catch him soon. Active players with the most NHL playoff goals (age in parentheses):

Joe Sakic (38) **82**

Jaromir Jagr (36) **72**

Peter Forsberg (34) **63**

Brendan Shanahan (39) **58**

Mike Modano (37) **53**

Source: NHL

By Kevin Greer and Alejandro Gonzalez, USA TODAY

USA TODAY Snapshots®

Better with age

After Mark O'Meara earned a green jacket in 1998, there has been a youth movement among Masters champions. The oldest champions at Augusta National since the 36-hole cut was instituted in 1957:

Jack Nicklaus (1986)	**46 years, 2 months**
Ben Crenshaw (1995)	**43 years, 2 months**
Gary Player (1978)	**42 years, 5 months**
Sam Snead (1954)	**41 years, 10 months**
Mark O'Meara (1998)	**41 years, 3 months**

Source: Masters.org

By Kevin Greer and Julie Snider, USA TODAY

USA TODAY Snapshots®

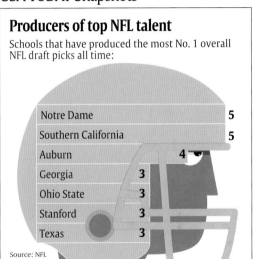

Producers of top NFL talent

Schools that have produced the most No. 1 overall NFL draft picks all time:

Notre Dame	5
Southern California	5
Auburn	4
Georgia	3
Ohio State	3
Stanford	3
Texas	3

Source: NFL

By Ellen J. Horrow and Adrienne Lewis, USA TODAY

USA TODAY Snapshots®

NBA teams sew up series

Teams who have won the most playoff series in the NBA all time:

93 — Los Angeles Lakers

66 — Boston Celtics

42 — Philadelphia 76ers

40 — New York Knicks

37 — Detroit Pistons

Note: Through 2007 playoffs.   Source: NBA

By Ellen J. Horrow and Alejandro Gonzalez, USA TODAY

USA TODAY Snapshots®

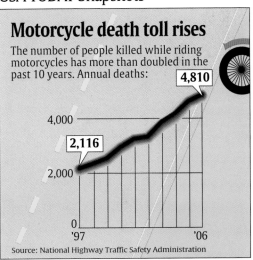

Motorcycle death toll rises

The number of people killed while riding motorcycles has more than doubled in the past 10 years. Annual deaths:

4,810

4,000

2,116

2,000

0

'97   '06

Source: National Highway Traffic Safety Administration

By Anne R. Carey and Adrienne Lewis, USA TODAY

▓ Holidays

What's your favorite thing about Thanksgiving? Do you look forward more to the food or to the family? Or do you dread the requisite travel too much to get very excited about either? How much do you spend on gifts for family? For friends? For co-workers? Who is the most difficult to shop for? How early do you start looking? Does that put you ahead of or behind the crowd?

Would you rather give or receive a present? What do you do with the gifts you'd rather not have gotten? Return them? Do you send holiday cards? Where do you display the ones sent to you? Do you write an annual newsletter? How do people really feel about reading holiday newsletters? How do you feel?

How do you fit in?

USA TODAY Snapshots®

People most difficult to buy gifts for

Everyone	28%
Adult men	27%
Adult women	21%
Teen boys	10%
Teen girls	10%
Children	1%
Babies	1%
Other	2%

Source: Harris Interactive online study via QuickQuery for Gifts.com of 2,730 adults, April 20–24. Margin of error ±3 percentage points.

By Mary Cadden and Sam Ward, USA TODAY

USA TODAY Snapshots®

Moms buy into Valentine's Day

The family member who gives the most Valentine's candy or other gifts:

33%

25%

16%

9%

18%

1%

| Mom/wife | Dad/husband | Children | Grand-parents | Pets | Other |

Source: Caravan Opinion Research Corporation survey of 1,000 adults for the National Confectioners Association, Nov. 30–Dec. 3. Margin of error ±3.1 percentage points.

By Mary Cadden and Alejandro Gonzalez, USA TODAY

USA TODAY Snapshots®

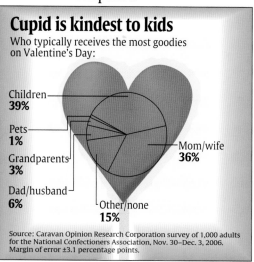

Cupid is kindest to kids

Who typically receives the most goodies on Valentine's Day:

Children
39%

Pets
1%

Grandparents
3%

Dad/husband
6%

Mom/wife
36%

Other/none
15%

Source: Caravan Opinion Research Corporation survey of 1,000 adults for the National Confectioners Association, Nov. 30–Dec. 3, 2006. Margin of error ±3.1 percentage points.

By Mary Cadden and Adrienne Lewis, USA TODAY

USA TODAY Snapshots®

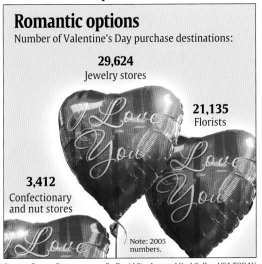

Romantic options

Number of Valentine's Day purchase destinations:

29,624
Jewelry stores

21,135
Florists

3,412
Confectionary
and nut stores

Note: 2005
numbers.

Source: Census Bureau   By David Stuckey and Karl Gelles, USA TODAY

USA TODAY Snapshots®

Would you let someone else do your gift shopping for you?

Yes
23%

No
77%

Source: Harris Interactive online study via QuickQuery for Gifts.com of 2,730 adults, April 20–24. Margin of error ±3 percentage points

By Mary Cadden and Bob Laird, USA TODAY

430

USA TODAY Snapshots®

Holiday finance

An average buyer will spend $603.86 this year for holiday gifts. How much the average buyer will spend for each group:

Family
$451.34

Friends
$85.60

Co-workers
$22.40

Others
$44.52

Source: National
Retail Federation

By Jae Yang and Sam Ward, USA TODAY

431

USA TODAY Snapshots®

Easter shopping

How much the average person who celebrates Easter spends for the holiday, top items:

Food
$37.56

Clothing
$26.03

Gifts
$20.61

Candy
$18.53

Flowers
$9.63

Source: BIGresearch   By Jae Yang and Bob Laird, USA TODAY

USA TODAY Snapshots®

Shopping for Mom

Where consumers will purchase Mother's Day gifts this year:

Specialty store (Florist, jeweler, etc.) — 37.5%

Department store — 29%

Discount store — 24%

Online — 20%

Specialty clothing store — 6.1%

Catalog — 2.9%

Note: Respondents could select more than one answer.

Source: National Retail Federation

By David Stuckey and Marcy E. Mullins, USA TODAY

USA TODAY Snapshots®

Mother's Day spending
Top gifts for Mother's Day and
average amount spent:

Flowers	**$19.98**
Jewelry	**$18.92**
Gift certificate	**$14.52**
Clothing	**$14.04**

Source: BIGresearch

By Jae Yang and Adrienne Lewis, USA TODAY

USA TODAY Snapshots®

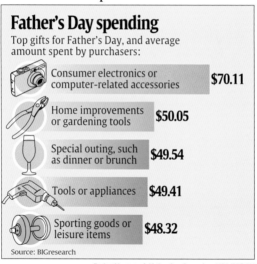

Father's Day spending

Top gifts for Father's Day, and average amount spent by purchasers:

Consumer electronics or computer-related accessories **$70.11**

Home improvements or gardening tools **$50.05**

Special outing, such as dinner or brunch **$49.54**

Tools or appliances **$49.41**

Sporting goods or leisure items **$48.32**

Source: BIGresearch

By Jae Yang and Alejandro Gonzalez, USA TODAY

USA TODAY Snapshots®

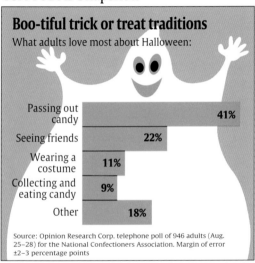

Boo-tiful trick or treat traditions

What adults love most about Halloween:

Passing out candy	41%
Seeing friends	22%
Wearing a costume	11%
Collecting and eating candy	9%
Other	18%

Source: Opinion Research Corp. telephone poll of 946 adults (Aug. 25–28) for the National Confectioners Association. Margin of error ±2–3 percentage points

By Mary Cadden and Sam Ward, USA TODAY

USA TODAY Snapshots®

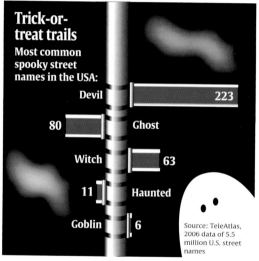

Trick-or-treat trails

Most common spooky street names in the USA:

Devil — 223
Ghost — 80
Witch — 63
Haunted — 11
Goblin — 6

Source: TeleAtlas, 2006 data of 5.5 million U.S. street names

By Mary Cadden and Julie Snider, USA TODAY

437

USA TODAY Snapshots®

Consumers spend more on Halloween

Average spending:

2003
$41.77

2007
$64.82

$60
$40
$20
0

'03 '04 '05 '06 '07

Source: BIGresearch survey of 8,877 respondents for the National Retail Federation. Margin of error ±1 percentage point.

By Karl Gelles and Jae Yang, USA TODAY

USA TODAY Snapshots®

Halloween shopping

How much consumers plan to spend, on average, on Halloween-related items:

Costumes
$23.33

Candy
$19.84

Decorations
$17.73

Greeting cards
$3.92

Combined average
$64.82

Source: BIGresearch survey of 8,877 respondents for the National Retail Federation. Margin of error ±1 percentage point.

By Jae Yang and Bob Laird, USA TODAY

USA TODAY Snapshots®

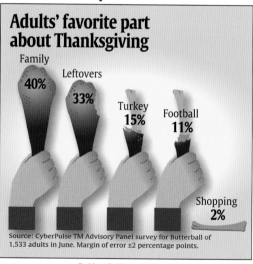

Adults' favorite part about Thanksgiving

Family
40%

Leftovers
33%

Turkey
15%

Football
11%

Shopping
2%

Source: CyberPulse TM Advisory Panel survey for Butterball of 1,533 adults in June. Margin of error ±2 percentage points.

By Mary Cadden and Alejandro Gonzalez, USA TODAY

USA TODAY Snapshots®

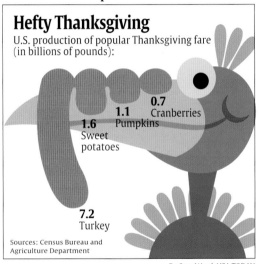

Hefty Thanksgiving
U.S. production of popular Thanksgiving fare (in billions of pounds):

0.7 Cranberries

1.1 Pumpkins

1.6 Sweet potatoes

7.2 Turkey

Sources: Census Bureau and Agriculture Department

By Sam Ward, USA TODAY

441

USA TODAY Snapshots®

Home for the holiday

How many miles adults plan to travel this Thanksgiving:

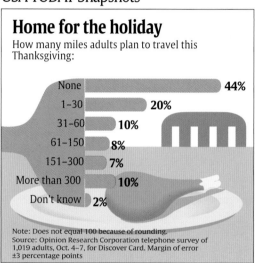

None	44%
1–30	20%
31–60	10%
61–150	8%
151–300	7%
More than 300	10%
Don't know	2%

Note: Does not equal 100 because of rounding.
Source: Opinion Research Corporation telephone survey of 1,019 adults, Oct. 4–7, for Discover Card. Margin of error ±3 percentage points

By Mary Cadden and Adrienne Lewis, USA TODAY

USA TODAY Snapshots®

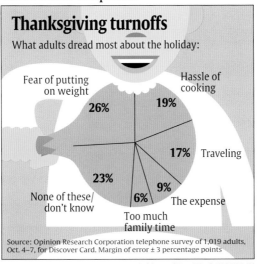

Thanksgiving turnoffs

What adults dread most about the holiday:

Fear of putting on weight
26%

Hassle of cooking
19%

17% Traveling

23%

None of these/ don't know

9%

6%

The expense

Too much family time

Source: Opinion Research Corporation telephone survey of 1,019 adults, Oct. 4–7, for Discover Card. Margin of error ± 3 percentage points

By Mary Cadden and Sam Ward, USA TODAY

USA TODAY Snapshots®

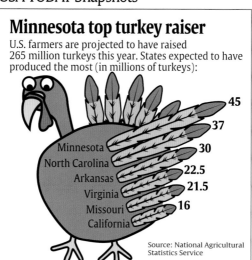

Minnesota top turkey raiser

U.S. farmers are projected to have raised 265 million turkeys this year. States expected to have produced the most (in millions of turkeys):

Minnesota — 45
North Carolina — 37
Arkansas — 30
Virginia — 22.5
Missouri — 21.5
California — 16

Source: National Agricultural Statistics Service

By Adrienne Lewis, USA TODAY

USA TODAY Snapshots®

Most holiday shoppers start in November

When do you start shopping for the holiday season?

Note: Total exceeds 100 due to rounding

14% Before Sept.

7% Sept.

20% Oct.

37% Nov.

19% First two weeks of Dec.

4% Last two weeks of Dec.

Source: National Retail Federation

By Jae Yang and Alejandro Gonzalez, USA TODAY

USA TODAY Snapshots®

Does your workload increase during the holidays?

Yes
28%

Stays the
same
42%

Don't
know
4%

Decrease
26%

Source: Accountemps survey
of 539 workers age 18 and
older. Margin of error ±4
percentage points.

By Jae Yang and Sam Ward, USA TODAY

USA TODAY Snapshots®

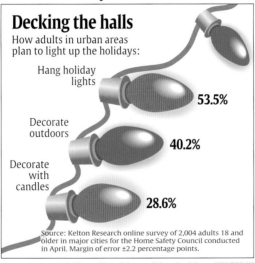

Decking the halls

How adults in urban areas
plan to light up the holidays:

Hang holiday
lights **53.5%**

Decorate
outdoors **40.2%**

Decorate
with
candles **28.6%**

Source: Kelton Research online survey of 2,004 adults 18 and
older in major cities for the Home Safety Council conducted
in April. Margin of error ±2.2 percentage points.

By Tracey Wong Briggs and Veronica Salazar, USA TODAY

USA TODAY Snapshots®

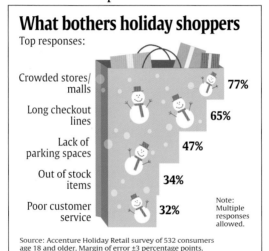

What bothers holiday shoppers

Top responses:

Crowded stores/malls **77%**

Long checkout lines **65%**

Lack of parking spaces **47%**

Out of stock items **34%**

Poor customer service **32%**

Note: Multiple responses allowed.

Source: Accenture Holiday Retail survey of 532 consumers age 18 and older. Margin of error ±3 percentage points.

By Jae Yang and Veronica Salazar, USA TODAY

USA TODAY Snapshots®

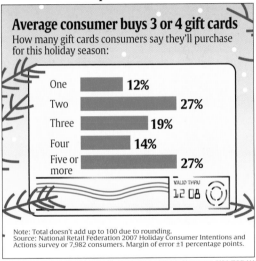

Average consumer buys 3 or 4 gift cards

How many gift cards consumers say they'll purchase for this holiday season:

One **12%**

Two **27%**

Three **19%**

Four **14%**

Five or more **27%**

VALID THRU
12 08

Note: Total doesn't add up to 100 due to rounding.
Source: National Retail Federation 2007 Holiday Consumer Intentions and Actions survey or 7,982 consumers. Margin of error ±1 percentage points.

By Jae Yang and Keith Simmons, USA TODAY

USA TODAY Snapshots®

Gift to keep

About 80% of gift givers sometimes enclose the receipt with their gifts. Did you return any gifts that you received in last year's holiday season?

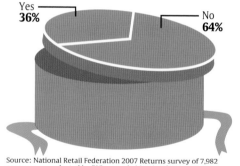

Yes
36%

No
64%

Source: National Retail Federation 2007 Returns survey of 7,982 consumers conducted by BIGresearch. Margin of error ±1 percentage points.

By Jae Yang and Adrienne Lewis, USA TODAY

USA TODAY Snapshots®

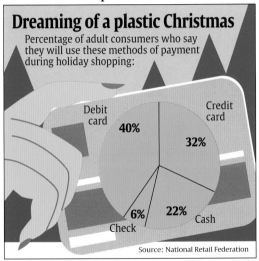

Dreaming of a plastic Christmas

Percentage of adult consumers who say they will use these methods of payment during holiday shopping:

Debit card **40%**

Credit card **32%**

6% Check

22% Cash

Source: National Retail Federation

By David Stuckey and Sam Ward, USA TODAY

451

USA TODAY Snapshots®

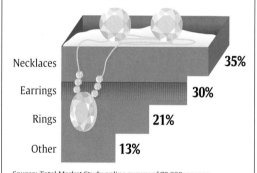

Diamonds under the tree

Women who got diamonds for Christmas last year received them in the form of:

Necklaces **35%**

Earrings **30%**

Rings **21%**

Other **13%**

Source: Total Market Study online survey of 72,000 women, ages 18 to 72 for the Diamond Informaiton Center. Margin of error ±1 percentage point.

By Mary Cadden and Veronica Salazar, USA TODAY

USA TODAY Snapshots®

Shopping for all ...
including yourself

Estimated average amount consumers plan to spend on holiday-related shopping for others and themselves.

Others
$620

Themselves
$107

Source: National Retail Federation

By David Stuckey and Sam Ward, USA TODAY

USA TODAY Snapshots®

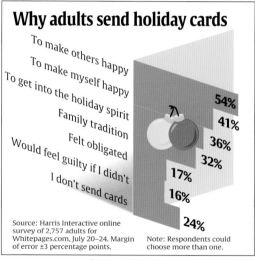

Why adults send holiday cards

To make others happy — 54%

To make myself happy — 41%

To get into the holiday spirit — 36%

Family tradition — 32%

Felt obligated — 17%

Would feel guilty if I didn't — 16%

I don't send cards — 24%

Source: Harris Interactive online survey of 2,757 adults for Whitepages.com, July 20–24. Margin of error ±3 percentage points.

Note: Respondents could choose more than one.

By Mary Cadden and Adrienne Lewis, USA TODAY

USA TODAY Snapshots®

Holiday newsletters are a mixed bag

Slightly more than half of adults like getting lengthy updates from family and friends

Like to receive — 51%

Do not like to receive — 44%

Not applicable — 5%

Source: Harris Interactive online survey of 2,757 adults for Whitepages.com, July 20–24. Margin of error ±3 percentage points.

By Mary Cadden and Alejandro Gonzalez, USA TODAY

USA TODAY Snapshots®

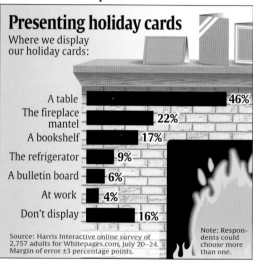

Presenting holiday cards

Where we display our holiday cards:

A table	46%
The fireplace mantel	22%
A bookshelf	17%
The refrigerator	9%
A bulletin board	6%
At work	4%
Don't display	16%

Source: Harris Interactive online survey of 2,757 adults for Whitepages.com, July 20–24. Margin of error ±3 percentage points.

Note: Respondents could choose more than one.

By Mary Cadden and Marcy E. Mullins , USA TODAY

USA TODAY Snapshots®

Poinsettia season

An estimated 70 million to 80 million poinsettias are usually sold during the holidays, making Christmas the top floral-buying holiday. Percentage of floral transactions, by holiday:

30%
Christmas/
Hanukkah

22%
Mother's
Day

18%
Valentine's
Day

15%
Easter/Passover

6%
Thanksgiving

Source:
www.about
flowers.com

By David Stuckey and Karl Gelles, USA TODAY

USA TODAY Snapshots®

Let's get real

Number of real Christmas trees purchased in 2005 compared with fake Christmas trees (in millions):

32.8

9.3

XMAS TREE

Real   Fake

Source: National Christmas Tree Association

By David Stuckey and Adrienne Lewis, USA TODAY

USA TODAY Snapshots®

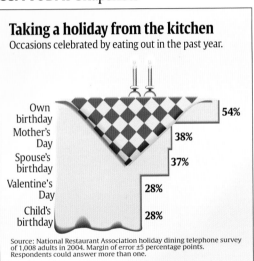

Taking a holiday from the kitchen
Occasions celebrated by eating out in the past year.

- Own birthday — **54%**
- Mother's Day — **38%**
- Spouse's birthday — **37%**
- Valentine's Day — **28%**
- Child's birthday — **28%**

Source: National Restaurant Association holiday dining telephone survey of 1,008 adults in 2004. Margin of error ±5 percentage points. Respondents could answer more than one.

By Mary Cadden and Robert W. Ahrens, USA TODAY

■ Health

If you could stay one age eternally, what age would you choose? What age do most women wish they could be? Are you taking measures to fight the aging process? How many men are electing to undergo cosmetic surgery? What procedures are most common? Would you go under the knife in the pursuit of beauty? Have you considered Botox? Have you ever had an injection?

What health conditions do you fear most? A heart attack? Diabetes? Cancer? What medical emergencies are most costly to treat? Do you take good care of your body in an effort at prevention? Did you get a flu vaccine this year? Do you exercise? Do you watch your diet? Is that normal? How many times have you resolved to lose weight this year? Are you insured? How many people are not?

How do you fare?

USA TODAY Snapshots®

Consumer nail-gun injuries spike

Nail-gun injuries to non-professional users treated in emergency rooms have risen as nail guns have become more accessible:

1993
5,299

1996
9,013

1999
11,947

2002
16,238

2005
13,378

Source: HJ Lipscomb and LL Jackson, Morbidity and Mortality Weekly Report; data from the National Electronic Injury Surveillance System, Consumer Products Safety Commission.

By Tracey Wong Briggs and Karl Gelles, USA TODAY

USA TODAY Snapshots®

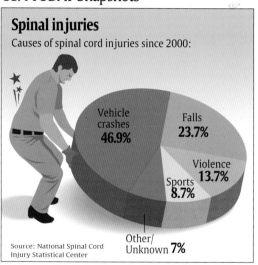

Spinal injuries

Causes of spinal cord injuries since 2000:

Vehicle crashes **46.9%**

Falls **23.7%**

Violence **13.7%**

Sports **8.7%**

Other/ Unknown **7%**

Source: National Spinal Cord Injury Statistical Center

By David Stuckey and Alejandro Gonzalez, USA TODAY

USA TODAY Snapshots®

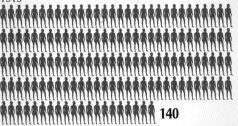

Decline of a deadly disease

Tuberculosis death rate in the USA (per 100,000 population):

1915

140

1967
3.5

2006
0.2

Source: Census Bureau

By David Stuckey and Alejandro Gonzalez, USA TODAY

USA TODAY Snapshots®

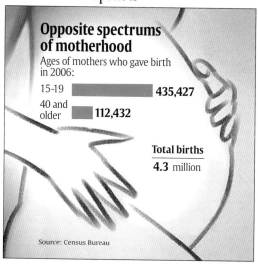

Opposite spectrums of motherhood

Ages of mothers who gave birth in 2006:

15-19 **435,427**

40 and older **112,432**

Total births

4.3 million

Source: Census Bureau

By David Stuckey and Keith Simmons, USA TODAY

USA TODAY Snapshots®

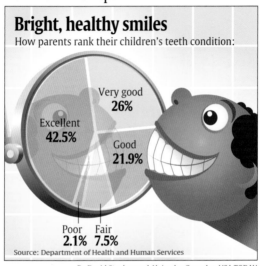

Bright, healthy smiles

How parents rank their children's teeth condition:

Very good
26%

Excellent
42.5%

Good
21.9%

Poor
2.1%

Fair
7.5%

Source: Department of Health and Human Services

By David Stuckey and Alejandro Gonzalez, USA TODAY

466

USA TODAY Snapshots®

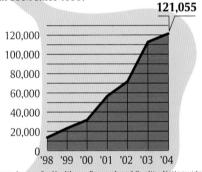

A boom in surgery for obesity

The number of people getting bariatric surgery, which includes gastric bypass, has risen more than 800% since 1998:

121,055

Sources: Agency for Healthcare Research and Quality, Nationwide Inpatient Sample, U.S. Department of Health and Human Services

By Tracey Wong Briggs and Sam Ward, USA TODAY

USA TODAY Snapshots®

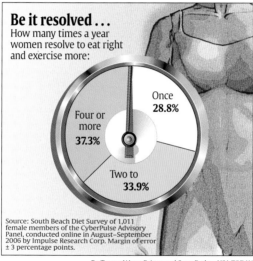

Be it resolved ...
How many times a year women resolve to eat right and exercise more:

Once
28.8%

Four or more
37.3%

Two to
33.9%

Source: South Beach Diet Survey of 1,011 female members of the CyberPulse Advisory Panel, conducted online in August–September 2006 by Impulse Research Corp. Margin of error ± 3 percentage points.

By Tracey Wong Briggs and Suzy Parker, USA TODAY

USA TODAY Snapshots®

Weight heavier on girls' minds

How important kids say it is to be a healthy weight:

Boys **Girls**

	Boys	Girls
Extremely important	24%	36%
Very important	26%	26%
Important	33%	27%
Somewhat important	12%	9%
Not at all important	4%	2%

Source: Harris Interactive online omnibus survey of 1,487 U.S. youth ages 8 to 18 Aug. 16-24 on behalf of America on the Move Foundation. Sampling error ±3 percentage points.

By Tracey Wong Briggs and Suzy Parker, USA TODAY

USA TODAY Snapshots®

How plastic surgery is shaping up

Cosmetic plastic surgery procedures have increased 48% over the past six years. The top five procedures in 2006 (in thousands):

Breast augmentation	329
Nose reshaping	307
Liposuction	303
Eyelid surgery	233
Tummy tuck	146

Source: American Society of Plastic Surgeons

By Mary Cadden and Adrienne Lewis, USA TODAY

USA TODAY Snapshots®

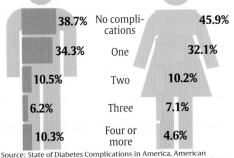

Diabetes gets complicated

Diabetic men are more likely than diabetic women to have complications. Percentage breakdown:

Men		Women
38.7%	No complications	45.9%
34.3%	One	32.1%
10.5%	Two	10.2%
6.2%	Three	7.1%
10.3%	Four or more	4.6%

Source: State of Diabetes Complications in America, American Association of Clinical Endocrinologists, citing 1999–2004 data from the Centers of Disease Control and Prevention

By Tracey Wong Briggs and Veronica Salazar, USA TODAY

USA TODAY Snapshots®

Making food healthier for kids

Should the government regulate "promoting" healthier diets for children, such as banning trans fats and certain foods?

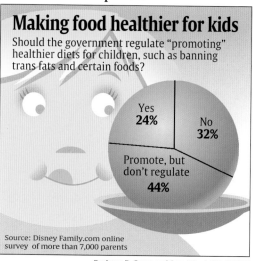

Yes
24%

No
32%

Promote, but don't regulate
44%

Source: Disney Family.com online survey of more than 7,000 parents

By Anne R. Carey and Sam Ward, USA TODAY

USA TODAY Snapshots®

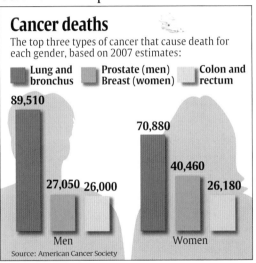

Cancer deaths

The top three types of cancer that cause death for each gender, based on 2007 estimates:

Lung and bronchus | Prostate (men) Breast (women) | Colon and rectum

Men
- 89,510
- 27,050
- 26,000

Women
- 70,880
- 40,460
- 26,180

Source: American Cancer Society

By Melanie Eversley and Marcy E. Mullins, USA TODAY

473

USA TODAY Snapshots®

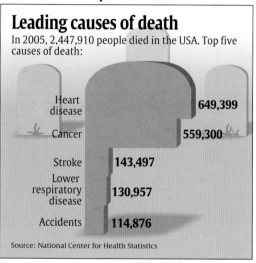

Leading causes of death

In 2005, 2,447,910 people died in the USA. Top five causes of death:

Heart disease	649,399
Cancer	559,300
Stroke	143,497
Lower respiratory disease	130,957
Accidents	114,876

Source: National Center for Health Statistics

By Adrienne Lewis, USA TODAY

USA TODAY Snapshots®

Costly medical conditions

The USA's five most expensive medical conditions cost about $320 billion to treat in 2005. Estimated spending for each condition (in billions):

Heart problems	**$76**
Trauma disorders (injuries from accidents and violence)	**$72**
Cancer	**$70**
Mental disorders, including depression	**$56**
Asthma and chronic obstructive pulmonary disease	**$54**

Note: Money paid for visits to doctors' offices, clinics and emergency departments, hospital stays, home health care and prescription medicines.

Source: Agency for Healthcare Research and Quality, Medical Expenditure Panel Survey

By Michelle Healy and Alejandro Gonzalez, USA TODAY

USA TODAY Snapshots®

A struggle to stay healthy

What U.S. adults say is the biggest challenge in achieving a healthy lifestyle:

Getting enough exercise **38%**

Getting enough sleep **34%**

Other **3%**

Eating a well-balanced diet **25%**

Source: KRC Research survey of 15,035 adults June 26-July 18 for Amway Global

By Anne R. Carey and Karl Gelles, USA TODAY

USA TODAY Snapshots®

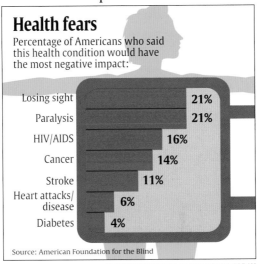

Health fears

Percentage of Americans who said this health condition would have the most negative impact:

Losing sight	21%
Paralysis	21%
HIV/AIDS	16%
Cancer	14%
Stroke	11%
Heart attacks/disease	6%
Diabetes	4%

Source: American Foundation for the Blind

By David Stuckey and Sam Ward, USA TODAY

USA TODAY Snapshots®

When does "old age" begin?

In general, Americans say old age begins around age 75. But that assessment shifts depending on the generation of the respondent:

80	77	74	69
Silent Generation (63 to 83)	Baby Boomers (44 to 62)	Generation X (32 to 43)	Generation Y (21 to 31)

Source: Rethinking Retirement survey of 3,866 adults ages 21-83 conducted by Harris Interactive for Charles Schwab with Age Wave

By Michelle Healy and Veronica Salazar, USA TODAY

USA TODAY Snapshots®

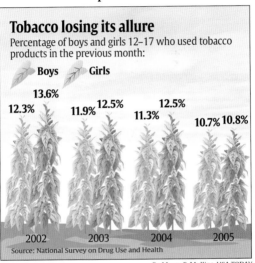

Tobacco losing its allure
Percentage of boys and girls 12–17 who used tobacco products in the previous month:

Boys   Girls

2002: 12.3% / 13.6%
2003: 11.9% / 12.5%
2004: 11.3% / 12.5%
2005: 10.7% / 10.8%

Source: National Survey on Drug Use and Health

By Marcy E. Mullins, USA TODAY

USA TODAY Snapshots®

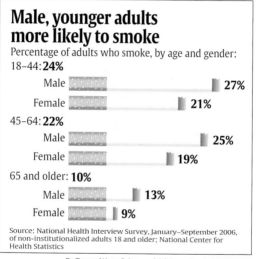

Male, younger adults more likely to smoke

Percentage of adults who smoke, by age and gender:

18–44: **24%**

Male **27%**

Female **21%**

45–64: **22%**

Male **25%**

Female **19%**

65 and older: **10%**

Male **13%**

Female **9%**

Source: National Health Interview Survey, January–September 2006, of non-institutionalized adults 18 and older; National Center for Health Statistics

By Tracey Wong Briggs and Adrienne Lewis, USA TODAY

USA TODAY Snapshots®

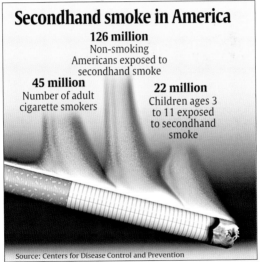

Secondhand smoke in America

126 million
Non-smoking
Americans exposed to
secondhand smoke

45 million
Number of adult
cigarette smokers

22 million
Children ages 3
to 11 exposed
to secondhand
smoke

Source: Centers for Disease Control and Prevention

By David Stuckey and Karl Gelles, USA TODAY

USA TODAY Snapshots®

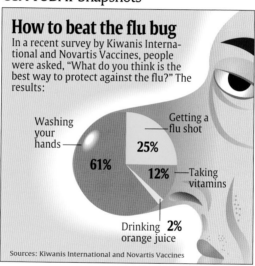

How to beat the flu bug

In a recent survey by Kiwanis International and Novartis Vaccines, people were asked, "What do you think is the best way to protect against the flu?" The results:

Washing your hands — **61%**

Getting a flu shot — **25%**

12% — Taking vitamins

Drinking orange juice **2%**

Sources: Kiwanis International and Novartis Vaccines

By David Stuckey and Alejandro Gonzalez, USA TODAY

USA TODAY Snapshots®

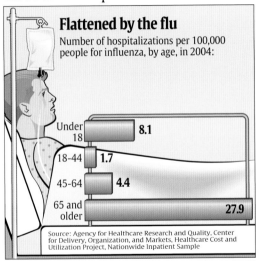

Flattened by the flu

Number of hospitalizations per 100,000 people for influenza, by age, in 2004:

Age	
Under 18	8.1
18-44	1.7
45-64	4.4
65 and older	27.9

Source: Agency for Healthcare Research and Quality, Center for Delivery, Organization, and Markets, Healthcare Cost and Utilization Project, Nationwide Inpatient Sample

By Tracey Wong Briggs and Marcy E. Mullins, USA TODAY

USA TODAY Snapshots®

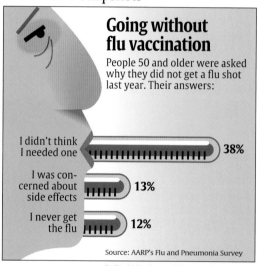

Going without flu vaccination

People 50 and older were asked why they did not get a flu shot last year. Their answers:

I didn't think I needed one — 38%

I was concerned about side effects — 13%

I never get the flu — 12%

Source: AARP's Flu and Pneumonia Survey

By David Stuckey and Sam Ward, USA TODAY

USA TODAY Snapshots®

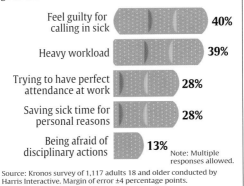

Working sick

Ninety-eight percent of survey respondents have gone to work when they were sick. Top reasons to go to work when sick:

Feel guilty for calling in sick **40%**

Heavy workload **39%**

Trying to have perfect attendance at work **28%**

Saving sick time for personal reasons **28%**

Being afraid of disciplinary actions **13%**

Note: Multiple responses allowed.

Source: Kronos survey of 1,117 adults 18 and older conducted by Harris Interactive. Margin of error ±4 percentage points.

By Jae Yang and Adrienne Lewis, USA TODAY

USA TODAY Snapshots®

Underage alcohol danger

Rates of emergency room visits among people ages 12–20 involving alcohol or alcohol combined with other drugs (per 100,000 population):

Males

Alcohol   **291**

Alcohol and drugs   **125**

Females

Alcohol   **223**

Alcohol and drugs   **115**

Source: Drug Abuse Warning Network

By David Stuckey and Karl Gelles, USA TODAY

486

USA TODAY Snapshots®

In recovery

Estimated number of members
of Alcoholics Anonymous:

1,190,637
USA

95,984
Canada

729,097
Outside USA
and Canada

Source: Alcoholics Anonymous

By David Stuckey and Alejandro Gonzalez, USA TODAY

USA TODAY Snapshots®

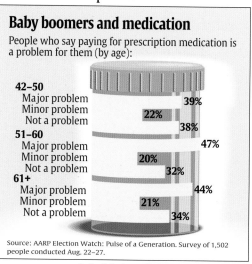

Baby boomers and medication

People who say paying for prescription medication is a problem for them (by age):

42–50
  Major problem — **39%**
  Minor problem — **22%**
  Not a problem — **38%**
51–60
  Major problem — **47%**
  Minor problem — **20%**
  Not a problem — **32%**
61+
  Major problem — **44%**
  Minor problem — **21%**
  Not a problem — **34%**

Source: AARP Election Watch: Pulse of a Generation. Survey of 1,502 people conducted Aug. 22–27.

By David Stuckey and Robert W. Ahrens, USA TODAY

USA TODAY Snapshots®

Where the drug dollars go

The five costliest classes of drugs accounted for two–thirds of the $181 billion spent on outpatient prescription drugs for adults in 2004. The top five, in billions spent:

Cardiovascular	$31.7
Hormones	$24.5
Central nervous system[1]	$23.7
Cholesterol-lowering	$21.5
Psychotherapeutics[2]	$17.9

1 — Including painkillers and seizure control drugs.
2 — Including antidepressants.
Source: Agency for Healthcare Research and Quality, Department of Health and Human Services

By Tracey Wong Briggs and Robert W. Ahrens, USA TODAY

USA TODAY Snapshots®

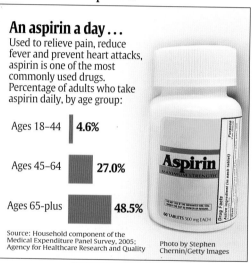

An aspirin a day . . .

Used to relieve pain, reduce fever and prevent heart attacks, aspirin is one of the most commonly used drugs. Percentage of adults who take aspirin daily, by age group:

Ages 18–44 **4.6%**

Ages 45–64 **27.0%**

Ages 65-plus **48.5%**

Source: Household component of the Medical Expenditure Panel Survey, 2005; Agency for Healthcare Research and Quality

Photo by Stephen Chernin/Getty Images

By Tracey Wong Briggs and Keith Simmons, USA TODAY

USA TODAY Snapshots®

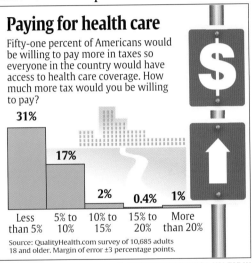

Paying for health care

Fifty-one percent of Americans would be willing to pay more in taxes so everyone in the country would have access to health care coverage. How much more tax would you be willing to pay?

31%

17%

2%

0.4%

1%

| Less than 5% | 5% to 10% | 10% to 15% | 15% to 20% | More than 20% |

Source: QualityHealth.com survey of 10,685 adults 18 and older. Margin of error ±3 percentage points.

By Jae Yang and Julie Snider, USA TODAY

USA TODAY Snapshots®

Insuring a family of four

The average cost of comprehensive health insurance for a family of four, including what an employee and a company pay, is about $11,000 per year. Do you think this is the right amount?

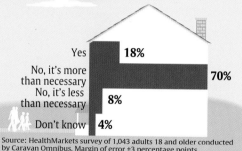

Yes **18%**

No, it's more than necessary **70%**

No, it's less than necessary **8%**

Don't know **4%**

Source: HealthMarkets survey of 1,043 adults 18 and older conducted by Caravan Omnibus. Margin of error ±3 percentage points.

By Jae Yang and Robert W. Ahrens, USA TODAY

USA TODAY Snapshots®

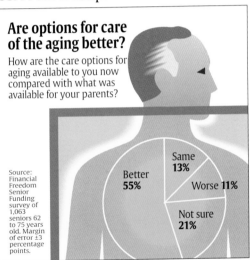

Are options for care of the aging better?

How are the care options for aging available to you now compared with what was available for your parents?

Source: Financial Freedom Senior Funding survey of 1,063 seniors 62 to 75 years old. Margin of error ±3 percentage points.

Better **55%**

Same **13%**

Worse **11%**

Not sure **21%**

By Jae Yang and and Bob Laird, USA TODAY

USA TODAY Snapshots®

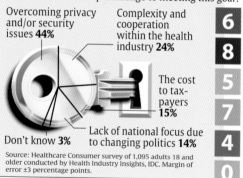

Electronic health records face security questions

The U.S. government wants electronic health records available to most U.S. citizens on a voluntary basis by 2014. What is the top challenge to meeting this goal?

Overcoming privacy and/or security issues **44%**

Complexity and cooperation within the health industry **24%**

The cost to tax-payers **15%**

Lack of national focus due to changing politics **14%**

Don't know **3%**

Source: Healthcare Consumer survey of 1,095 adults 18 and older conducted by Health Industry Insights, IDC. Margin of error ±3 percentage points.

By Jae Yang and Bob Laird, USA TODAY

USA TODAY Snapshots®

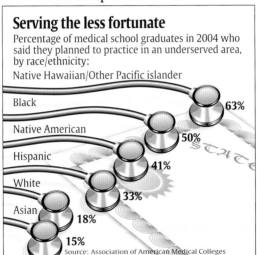

Serving the less fortunate

Percentage of medical school graduates in 2004 who said they planned to practice in an underserved area, by race/ethnicity:

Native Hawaiian/Other Pacific islander

Black — **63%**

Native American — **50%**

Hispanic — **41%**

White — **33%**

Asian — **18%**

15%

Source: Association of American Medical Colleges

By David Stuckey and Marcy E. Mullins, USA TODAY

USA TODAY Snapshots®

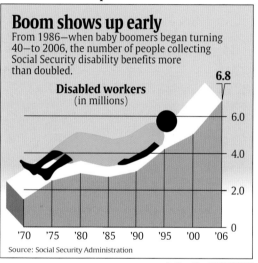

Boom shows up early

From 1986—when baby boomers began turning 40—to 2006, the number of people collecting Social Security disability benefits more than doubled.

Disabled workers
(in millions)

6.8

6.0

4.0

2.0

0

'70   '75   '80   '85   '90   '95   '00   '06

Source: Social Security Administration

By Sam Ward, USA TODAY

USA TODAY Snapshots®

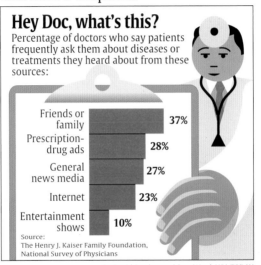

Hey Doc, what's this?

Percentage of doctors who say patients frequently ask them about diseases or treatments they heard about from these sources:

Source	Percentage
Friends or family	37%
Prescription-drug ads	28%
General news media	27%
Internet	23%
Entertainment shows	10%

Source:
The Henry J. Kaiser Family Foundation,
National Survey of Physicians

By David Stuckey and Sam Ward, USA TODAY

USA TODAY Snapshots®

What's up doc?
Top five issues that parents consider very important for health care providers to discuss with adolescents:

77%
67%
61%
57%
54%

Diet/nutrition
Exercise/sports
Physical changes of puberty
Drug use
Tobacco use

Source: Knowledge Networks survey of 2,060 adults for the C.S. Mott Children's Hospital National Poll on Children's Health.

By Michelle Healy and Dave Merrill, USA TODAY

USA TODAY Snapshots®

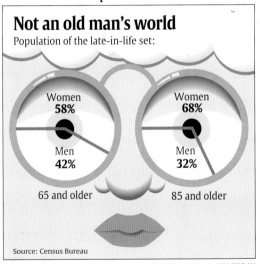

Not an old man's world

Population of the late-in-life set:

Women **58%**

Men **42%**

65 and older

Women **68%**

Men **32%**

85 and older

Source: Census Bureau

By Adrienne Lewis, USA TODAY

USA TODAY Snapshots®

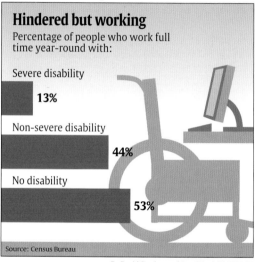

Hindered but working

Percentage of people who work full time year-round with:

Severe disability

13%

Non-severe disability

44%

No disability

53%

Source: Census Bureau

By David Stuckey and Sam Ward, USA TODAY

USA TODAY Snapshots®

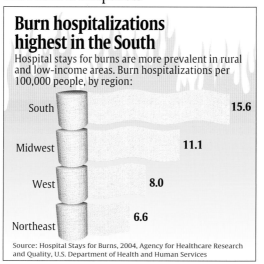

Burn hospitalizations highest in the South

Hospital stays for burns are more prevalent in rural and low-income areas. Burn hospitalizations per 100,000 people, by region:

South **15.6**

Midwest **11.1**

West **8.0**

Northeast **6.6**

Source: Hospital Stays for Burns, 2004, Agency for Healthcare Research and Quality, U.S. Department of Health and Human Services

By Tracey Wong Briggs and Marcy E. Mullins, USA TODAY

USA TODAY Snapshots®

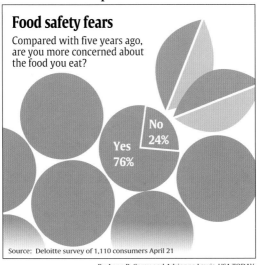

Food safety fears

Compared with five years ago, are you more concerned about the food you eat?

Yes
76%

No
24%

Source: Deloitte survey of 1,110 consumers April 21

By Anne R. Carey and Adrienne Lewis, USA TODAY

USA TODAY Snapshots®

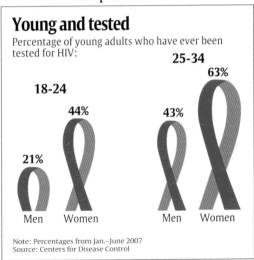

Young and tested

Percentage of young adults who have ever been tested for HIV:

18-24

25-34

21% Men

44% Women

43% Men

63% Women

Note: Percentages from Jan.–June 2007
Source: Centers for Disease Control

By David Stuckey and Adrienne Lewis, USA TODAY

USA TODAY Snapshots®

Tired of snoring

About 46% of spouses/partners of snorers say they lose a good night's sleep at least a few nights a month. Sleep lost on nights the snoring is disruptive:

1 hour or less **51%**

28% 2 hours

21%

3 hours or more

Source: Breathe Right Nasal Strips survey of 800 snorers and their partners

By Anne R. Carey and Sam Ward, USA TODAY

USA TODAY Snapshots®

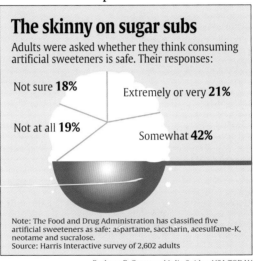

The skinny on sugar subs

Adults were asked whether they think consuming artificial sweeteners is safe. Their responses:

Not sure **18%**

Extremely or very **21%**

Not at all **19%**

Somewhat **42%**

Note: The Food and Drug Administration has classified five artificial sweeteners as safe: aspartame, saccharin, acesulfame-K, neotame and sucralose.
Source: Harris Interactive survey of 2,602 adults

By Anne R. Carey and Julie Snider, USA TODAY

USA TODAY Snapshots®

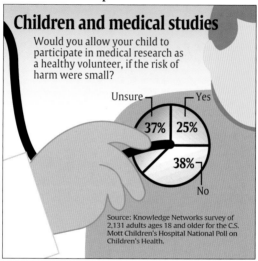

Children and medical studies

Would you allow your child to participate in medical research as a healthy volunteer, if the risk of harm were small?

Unsure — 37%
Yes — 25%
No — 38%

Source: Knowledge Networks survey of 2,131 adults ages 18 and older for the C.S. Mott Children's Hospital National Poll on Children's Health.

By Michelle Healy and Keith Simmons, USA TODAY

506

USA TODAY Snapshots®

Breast cancer
Estimated new breast cancer cases and total breast cancer deaths in 2007:

Estimated
new cases
180,510

Deaths
40,910

Source: American Cancer Society

By David Stuckey and Alejandro Gonzalez, USA TODAY

USA TODAY Snapshots®

Health insurance and alternative medicine

Do you believe health insurance should cover alternative medicine techniques such as chiropractic, nutrition counseling, acupuncture and osteopathy?

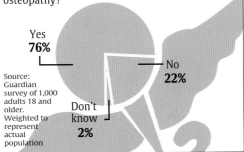

Yes
76%

No
22%

Don't know
2%

Source: Guardian survey of 1,000 adults 18 and older. Weighted to represent actual population

By Jae Yang and Adrienne Lewis, USA TODAY

USA TODAY Snapshots®

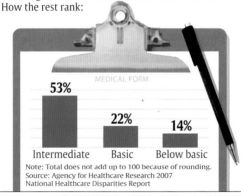

Health care literacy

Just twelve percent of American adults are considered proficient enough to fill out complex medical forms and weigh the risks and benefits of various treatments. How the rest rank:

MEDICAL FORM

53% Intermediate
22% Basic
14% Below basic

Note: Total does not add up to 100 because of rounding.
Source: Agency for Healthcare Research 2007
National Healthcare Disparities Report

By Michelle Healy and Alejandro Gonzalez, USA TODAY

Members of the USA TODAY Snapshots® **Team**

"I saw it in USA TODAY."

Four new Snapshots® delivered to your door every day.

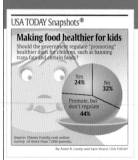

USA TODAY Snapshots®

Making food healthier for kids

Should the government regulate "promoting" healthier diets for children, such as banning trans fats and certain foods?

Yes
24%

No
32%

Promote, but
don't regulate
44%

Source: Disney Family.com online survey of more than 7,000 parents.

By Anne R. Carey and Sam Ward, USA TODAY

For home or office delivery, visit
usatodaysubscribe.com

REFERENCE

$12.95
Can. $13.95

DID YOU KNOW THAT
ACCORDING TO USA TODAY SNAPSHOTS®,

15% OF AMERICAN WOMEN OWN MORE THAN 30 PAIRS OF SHOES?

31% OF ADULTS SAY THEY OFTEN FALL ASLEEP IN BORING BUSINESS MEETINGS?

MINNESOTA FARMERS ARE THE TOP TURKEY RAISERS IN THE COUNTRY?

These are only 3 of the more than 2,000 fun facts, figures, and opinions you'll find in this entertaining and informative book compiled from USA TODAY Snapshots®, the popular feature found in the country's most widely read newspaper.

Dip in and out of these irresistibly engaging pages for a fascinating look at what the country thinks about technology, leisure, sports, and so much more.

STERLING INNOVATION
An imprint of Sterling Publishing Co., Inc.

New York / London
www.sterlingpublishing.com

ISBN 978-1-4027-6438-7

51295>

9 781402 764387